The Other Side of the Boat

Nancy Neuharth Troyer

ISBN 13: 978-0-8163-2623-5
ISBN 10: 0-8163-2623-1

Dedication

WE WERE ALWAYS HOME

This book is dedicated to "the wind beneath my wings."

For the past forty-plus, years I have been blessed to be the
wife and traveling companion of

CHAPLAIN DONALD E. TROYER,
LTC U.S.A. Retired.

Together with our beloved daughter "Steph,"
we have traveled the globe,
living in Thailand, Germany, Korea,
and the states of Michigan, Georgia, Tennessee, Oklahoma,
Kansas, New Jersey, Texas, and California.

Wherever we were together, we were always home.

I love you, Don!

Acknowledgments

The author gratefully acknowledges the following persons for their invaluable assistance in the preparation of this book:

To my father, Ruben Neuharth, who encouraged my husband and me throughout our years of ministry in far-flung places, resulting in the articles that chronicled my experiences. He supervised the compilation of the stories from the archives.

To my brother, Dennis, who assisted in the compilation of the stories and helped to convert them from hard copy files into digital documents all the way from Missouri, his home at the outset of the project.

To Bob Vincent, retired newspaper editor and family friend for more than fifty-five years, who developed the chapter concept of the book and wrote the introduction, prologue, and epilogue. He also edited and formatted the text.

To my mother, the late Nancy Hutchinson Neuharth, my brother Gary and his family, and Dennis's family and many friends and church associates for their encouragement and prayers along the way.

Introduction

Where can I go from Your Spirit? Or where can I flee from Your presence?
If I ascend into heaven, You are there; if I make my bed in hell, behold,
You are there. If I take the wings of the morning, and dwell in the
uttermost parts of the sea, even there Your hand shall lead me, and Your
right hand shall hold me.   —*Psalm 139: 7–10, NKJV*

The Bible contains numerous references attesting to the omnipresence of
God. The text from Psalm 139, a portion of which is printed here, is one of the
most prominent and surely one of the most beautifully worded examples.

After the psalmist, King David, experienced this truth personally, it led him
to place every aspect of his life in God's hands.

The prophet Jonah had to discover the hard way that God is not confined
and that He exists everywhere. When God gave Jonah an assignment he didn't
want to undertake, he reacted differently from how David would have. Jonah
1:1–3 sets the stage for the prophet's awakening: "Now the word of the LORD
came to Jonah the son of Amittai, saying, 'Arise, go to Nineveh, that great city,
and cry out against it; for their wickedness has come up before Me.' But Jonah
arose to flee to Tarshish from the presence of the LORD. He went down to Joppa,
and found a ship going to Tarshish; so he paid the fare, and went down into it, to
go with them to Tarshish from the presence of the LORD" (NKJV).

It was a commonly held belief by many in those days (792–753 B.C.) that
a ship would drop off the earth if it sailed too close to the edge, and Tarshish
(thought to be modern-day Gibraltar on the southern tip of Spain) was the
farthest distance from Palestine known to the Israelites.

The story of Jonah is a familiar one to most people and illustrates, among
other lessons, that God, as Creator of everything, is Sovereign, Omnipotent,
Omniscient, and Omnipresent and never can be limited by human misconcep-
tions.

Nancy Ann Neuharth Troyer (known affectionately as "Nan" by her family
and close friends) already was well grounded in her faith in God through Jesus
Christ when she attended and was graduated from Andrews University in
Berrien Springs, Michigan. It was there that she met Donald Eugene Troyer in

the autumn of 1968. They eloped a year and a half later on Valentine's Day in 1970, launching more than forty years of travel and adventure around the world for Nan as an army chaplain's wife.

Early in her adult life, Nan acquired the nickname "The Notetaker." Here is her explanation of how this came about:

"I found myself at times falling asleep in embarrassing situations—waiting for a traffic light to change, in meetings, and, heaven forbid, even in church! My doctor ruled out sleep apnea, but he advised, among other things, that I keep my mind busy in physically quiet moments. I began taking notes on various things, including sermons. That's when I picked up the 'Notetaker' tag."

The Troyers gained a greater understanding and appreciation of such Bible promises as "Therefore do not worry, saying, 'What shall we eat?' or 'What shall we drink?' or 'What shall we wear?' For after all these things the Gentiles seek. For your heavenly Father knows that you need all these things. But seek first the kingdom of God and His righteousness, and all these things shall be added to you. Therefore do not worry about tomorrow, for tomorrow will worry about its own things. Sufficient for the day is its own trouble" (Matthew 6:31–34, NKJV); "And we know that all things work together for good to those who love God, to those who are the called according to His purpose" (Romans 8:28, NKJV).

Experience after experience—all carefully logged into her ever-present notebook—proved over and over that no matter where they lived, God was there watching, guiding, protecting, encouraging, and comforting in times of danger and difficulty, and smiling during times of rejoicing.

Nancy used her extensive notes to record how God has worked in her life and in the lives of her family members. She wrote accounts of these experiences, most of them tied together with Scripture verses that parallel the life incidents, and these later appeared in newsletters and correspondence under the heading, "Nancy's Notes From the Other Side."

Since many of the articles concerned experiences abroad, the title appropriately could apply to stories from the other side of the globe. She developed the name, however, from an incident recorded in Luke 5:1–11, when Jesus had gone to the shores of Lake Gennesaret in quest of disciples. He called out to some fishermen who were washing their nets after toiling all night without catching anything. He told them to cast again on *the other side* of the boat. Peter told Him about their lack of success, but agreed to do what Jesus said. They threw out the nets on the right side and caught so many fish that the nets began to break. Jesus then told them that thereafter they would be fishers of men.

This collection of personal experiences in many areas of human emotions and life situations provides a glimpse of how living on "the other side" can reveal the beautiful and many times unexpected ways that Jesus is able to surprise those who have faith in what He can and will do for His children. These testimonies developed by the author over years of such experiences will inspire, encourage, comfort, and uplift you and help you gain confirmation of His presence all around you.

Nan emphasizes that it is important to remember that God doesn't always take away our problems, but He does give us grace and strength to deal with them. It also is important, she adds, to have faith that Someone is watching out for you, even when it may not seem that way. When things don't appear to be going your way, "Look for 'the good' that is promised in Romans 8:28," she recommends.

Nan and Chaplain Don Troyer, Lieutenant Colonel U.S. Army (retired) live in Banning, California. If you would like to communicate with her, the email address is Nan7Banner@aol.com. In the subject line put "Nancy's Notes."

Robert O. Vincent
Santa Paula, California
Spring 2011

Prologue

It would be difficult to associate the word *ordinary* with almost any phase of the extraordinary life of Nancy Ann Neuharth Troyer. In retrospect, she could see the hand of God guiding her through every experience, in good times and not-so-good times—and there was an abundance of both.

Her experiences demonstrate a firm conviction that God delivers on the promise in Romans 8:28, where Paul declares, "And we know that all things work together for good to them that love God, to them who are the called according to his purpose."

The Other Side of the Boat is a collection of more than one hundred accounts of those life experiences that illustrate and reinforce this promise while reaffirming the convictions of David in Psalm 139 attesting to the omnipotence, omniscience, and omnipresence of God. As the wife of Army Chaplain Don Troyer, who had achieved the rank of lieutenant colonel at the time of his retirement in 2000, she has lived and worked in many remote parts of the world during this thirty-year ministry and beyond.

Let's go back about six-and-a-half decades to see when, where, and how all this started.

Nancy was born on August 4, 1945, to Ruben and Nancy Marie (Hutchinson) Neuharth in Pittsburg, California, where her father was secretary-manager of the Chamber of Commerce at the beginning of a long and illustrious career as chief executive officer of business associations also in National City, Inglewood (where he served for seventeen years) and Escondido. She was the Neuharths' third child, preceded by sons Gary in 1938 and Dennis in 1939. A younger brother, Steven, born in 1952, and his bride of seven days died in a traffic accident in Ogallala, Nebraska, in 1975.

"I was born during the closing days of World War II," Nancy says, adding that Pittsburg was a departure point for military personnel who were shipping out for duty in the Pacific. "Ironically, my future father-in-law shipped out from Pittsburg. My mother remembers the grief showing in the faces of the soldiers as they marched past our house to their waiting ships."

Her preschool years were spent in California's fabled Napa Valley, where her family lived in the small hill community of Angwin. She attended first grade in

National City, followed by a move to Inglewood where she enrolled in the Inglewood Adventist Junior Academy for grades 2 through 10. Grades 11 and 12 were at Lynwood Academy in that suburban Los Angeles community.

Nancy gave her heart to Christ and was baptized when she was nine years old, after studying the basic tenets of her Adventist faith. "At the time, others in the church looked a little askance at such a young baptism, but I remember it like it was yesterday. I know I was so much more caring at school than I had been before, as if I had a helper walking beside me and guiding me through the moments of my young life. And of course, I did and do have a Helper—Jesus Christ!" She credits her mother's unselfish heart and happy spirit with sustaining her in her Christian walk.

I first met Ruben Neuharth in 1952 when he became the chief executive of the Inglewood, California, Chamber of Commerce. I was managing editor of the *Inglewood Daily News* and worked closely with him in the area of community and business affairs. Because we had three daughters who were close in age to the Neuharth children, we also associated socially, more so when we became next-door neighbors in 1957. Many times we would gather in the Neuharth family room and sing gospel songs. I could see that Nancy had more than ordinary musical talent even as a preteen. Time proved that she developed that and other artistic abilities to a high degree of perfection and has used them well in personal development as well as Christian ministry.

"My employment history before college included working for Dad at the Chamber of Commerce in Inglewood," Nancy says. "My first job was janitor, sweeping up in the evenings after closing time. Later I graduated to Girl Friday, helping out wherever I was needed—stuffing envelopes, running the Mimeograph machine, stamping letters, designing brochures, and hostessing social events.

"I really loved the job because I was able to meet community leaders, be of help to Dad, and work alongside the experienced office secretaries like Annette, Lee, and Peggy. I really learned a lot from them."

On top of all that, "I had the opportunity to earn money before I was fully skilled," Nancy adds.

After graduation from Lynwood Academy, Nancy was not certain what the immediate future held. "It's a minor miracle that I got to go to college at all," she says. "Dad felt women didn't need to go to college. He relented when a close friend persuaded him that it would be a wise move."

Nancy's first choice for her advanced education was Pacific Union College in northern California. "First of all, it was one of our church's (Adventist) colleges. And second, my brother Dennis was still a student there," said Nancy, adding, "It was located in Angwin where we owned land on the mountain above Napa, and the folks still had the dream of building a home and moving back there."

At Pacific Union College (PUC), Nancy enjoyed participating in talent contests where she gave readings, one of which was a Joan of Arc soliloquy she had written herself. "My professor, John George, felt I had plagiarized the piece. I was aghast! I would never even think about doing that. I did get some grammatical help from my brother Dennis, but nothing else." Displaying her humorous side, Nancy also gave, on several occasions, recitations from Victor Borge's acclaimed "Phonetic Punctuation" skit.

Building on skills learned in earlier job training, Nancy continued to gain experience and earn money while at PUC by working first as a switchboard operator, Speech Department secretary, and library file clerk. She also was a grocery store "cookie-cracker stacker" and door-to-door Bible salesperson. During the summers, she worked at a youth camp near Yosemite National Park.

While Nancy was at PUC, she met a young man named Doug who was planning to attend seminary following graduation. He invited her to go with him to Andrews University in Berrien Springs, Michigan, the home of the only Seventh-day Adventist Church seminary, along with its undergraduate and graduate programs. She made plans to enroll at Andrews.

"With the permission of my parents, Doug and I traveled together to Michigan," she says. "The school has a beautiful campus and Michigan was my first experience at really dramatic changes of seasons. My poetic heart loved it! I continued my major in speech and dabbled in art as well."

Doug and Nancy arrived in late summer of 1967 when the seminary classes started. "But by the time my classes started in the fall, we had parted ways. I was depressed at first but then found that I enjoyed mingling with the internationals in seminary and graduate school at meals in the cafeteria and elsewhere. This was a pure adventure for this California gal!" she says.

In recalling some of her memorable moments after coming to Andrews University, she concedes that some were not totally academic in nature. "I remember rolling up in a large rug in the girls' dorm, apparently trying to be a part of the building. Yep! Check me into a mental ward."

On another occasion, presumably for the purpose of studying mob actions, "I crawled out of the dorm's basement window to attend a protest for who-knows-what one evening where water hoses were used to disperse the rollicking crowd of college students. While trying to sneak back in, I met the dean at the door." You can make up your own ending to that story.

It was in the autumn of 1968 that Nancy first met her future husband. A classmate, now Dr. Nanette Wuchenich, invited her to come with her to listen to the University Singers as they practiced. Don was a member of the group.

"It was perhaps around Thanksgiving because there was snow on the ground," she recalls. "Meeting Don was like walking into another room. There he was on the top row, singing his heart out and smiling from ear to ear. He loved music and still does."

After the rehearsal, Nanette, Don, and Nancy were walking toward a restaurant for a snack when they came upon an accident scene. A car had run up on the curb near the girls' dorm and had sustained a flat tire. Don excused himself and went over to help.

"I saw compassion in him and remembered it," Nancy says. "Since then I have learned what an unselfish person Don really is. He comes from a Mennonite background and that kindness is instilled in him. He is very observant and is a good judge of character."

Their first date was at a Valentine's Day banquet in 1969. Don was a senior business major and Nancy had a year to go until she would graduate.

"During the evening at the banquet, Don pulled out his wallet and showed me a picture of his family, mentioning at the same time that his father and brother were morticians," Nan recalls. "Ugh! They looked so pasty white, I thought as I looked at the photograph. I discovered later that they weren't, really. Actually they were very talkative and engaging. But my first impressions were not positive."

Donald Eugene Troyer was born in Three Rivers, Michigan, a year before Nancy was, and he grew up in Indiana. As noted earlier, his religious background was Mennonite. He had three uncles who were Mennonite ministers. His maternal grandmother, Gladys Monroe, was introduced to Adventism by her brother, and eventually Don's family changed faiths, but he has never forgotten the kindness of his Mennonite friends and family.

Don was drafted into the army following graduation from Andrews University. "The lottery number system had not yet been put into effect by the Selective Service system," Nancy says. "His draft number was in the 300s, and if the draft had been operating under the lottery, with a number that high he probably wouldn't have been called in 1969. But God knew best."

On February 14, 1970, the anniversary of their first date, a momentous moment came in the lives of Nancy and Don. She was a senior at the university and Don was a soldier in the army.

"We eloped," says Nancy. "It was a silly thing to do, but we did it. I don't remember thinking about it at the time, and it had nothing to do with our decision, but at Christmastime in 1935, my parents also eloped to Reno, Nevada. Mom was living in Lodi, California, at the time and Dad was on Christmas break from the army and navy academy in Carlsbad, near San Diego. So here we were in an identical situation—eloping during schooltime far away from home."

Don and Nancy's marriage wasn't a typical elopement. "We were married in a little Methodist church in White Pigeon, Michigan. It was the same church where Don's parents and grandparents were married in two other wars, and both were in attendance at our wedding."

Nancy graduated a few months afterward and Don was assigned to Fort Benning, Georgia, where they set up their first home in nearby Columbus.

Don surrendered to Christ early in his military career at a chapel service. "He was led to the Lord by some pretty remarkable chaplains, and he never forgot them," said Nancy.

In 1971, Don was deployed for a tour of duty in Bangkok, Thailand, with a detour to Vietnam, and was joined later by Nancy. Don extended his military commitment to a four-year enlistment and was assigned to work with Chaplain Conrad "Connie" N. Walker (Colonel) in the U.S. Army Support Command in the United States, headed by four-star General John W. Vessey Jr., a highly decorated hero of World War II, Korea, and Vietnam.

Colonel Walker, himself something of a military legend and title figure in the book *The Leapin' Deacon,* which tells of his heroic exploits under hostile conditions in Vietnam, showed Don that a chaplain can encourage and nurture soldiers in their faith. He recommended that Don join the ranks of Army chaplains. Colonel Walker is now retired and lives in San Antonio, Texas. "We are still good friends and brethren in Christ," Nancy comments.

When Don's enlistment was up, the Troyers headed back to Berrien Springs where he enrolled in the seminary at Andrews University preparatory to becoming a minister. This was the first step toward a future in the chaplaincy. Two years later they moved to Savannah, Georgia, as associate pastor. Subsequently, he was associate pastor in Atlanta (1976-77) and Macon (1977) before accepting his first assignment as a head pastor at Thomasville and Barwick (1977-79). They moved to Hixson, Tennessee, where he served until 1980 when he reentered military service, now as an officer and chaplain. All the while, Nancy was at his side.

He was assigned to Fort Sill, Oklahoma, which marked his entry into the army chaplaincy. It was there that a beautiful child came into their lives early in May 1982. They made a fast trip to Dalton, Georgia, to pick up Stephanie Dawn Troyer and return her to their home in Lawton, Oklahoma, near Fort Sill, where they remained until 1983 when Don was assigned to Spangdahlem Air Force Base in the Mosel Valley of central Germany. The now-three Troyer family members lived in nearby Herforst from 1983 to 1986.

Nancy tells the full, touching story of how Stephanie came into their lives in the article "Spinning Miracles" elsewhere in this book.

After the three years in Germany, Don was reassigned to chaplaincy posts in the United States, first at Fort Monmouth, New Jersey, followed by Fort Benning, Fort Leavenworth (Kansas), and back to Fort Monmouth before deployment to Seoul, Korea, from 1994 to 1995. He then returned to Fort Gillem, Georgia, for two years, followed by a three-year assignment at Fort Hood, Texas, where he retired from military service in 2000 after thirty years.

"Don was at the peak of his military career," Nancy says. "He was the Garrison Chaplain at Fort Hood, responsible for the support of ten chapels and more than ninety chaplains. Later he was the Garrison Troop Chaplain, working side by side with the installation chaplain at retirement. The Chief of Chaplains had encouraged Don to stay on, but his health was deteriorating and our daughter was having problems in high school so we felt it was a good time to move on."

It needs to be noted that most of the time Nancy was with Don at military bases both in the United States and abroad, and she was gainfully employed in a number of occupations, helping with family expenses and gaining valuable experience while gathering new entries for her notebook.

Among the part-time or short-term jobs she held between the time they were married and Don's retirement from the army were teaching speech and English at a mission school in Thailand, serving as secretary for several seminary professors at Andrews University, a Kelly Girl in Atlanta, a nursing home receptionist, homeschooling mom for four years, director of a servicemen's center in Korea, school secretary-receptionist, and "limo" driver and recreation assistant at an active senior retirement center.

After Don's army retirement, the opportunity arose to continue to work with military personnel in a less demanding job in Europe through the Adventist Church.

"So in February of 2000," Nancy says, "Don, Stephanie, and I left Texas aboard a jet plane bound for Germany where Don would become the director of the Adventist Military Support Center in Frankfurt. It was an easy transition from military life because we were supporting the military members and their families who visited the servicemen's center—a sort of bed and breakfast and Adventist recreation facility," Nancy says, adding, "I juggled two jobs—one as hostess for the center, writing a weekly email newsletter, cooking meals on weekends for a big Saturday night potluck, and hosting overnight guests; and second as front-desk clerk at the Rhein Main Air Force Base Hotel in Frankfurt. It was a part-time job that entitled us to keep military privileges while in Europe. I worked about three days a week checking in military personnel and others. At times it was a stressful job, but never boring. I was able to write several stories about events at the hotel."

Nancy's experience as the principal director of the International Servicemen's Center in Seoul, Korea, in 1994 and 1995, made her extremely qualified for her work at the Adventist Center.

With Frankfurt as home base, Don and Nancy were able to see a lot of Europe, mostly while traveling to military bases to visit with Adventist worship leaders in England, Italy, Spain, and other distant localities. Many of Nancy's adventures in Europe are chronicled in this book.

When the assignment in Germany was concluded in July of 2002, the Troyers returned to the home they owned in Stockbridge, Georgia, in the mid-nineties. "We hadn't been able to sell it when we were transferred to Texas in 1997, so we rented it to a fine Christian couple for five years," Nancy explains.

They lived there until 2003, when Don reentered the pastoral ministry at Auburn and Athens, Georgia. Concurrently, Nancy worked as the district newsletter editor, producing a weekly four-page letter distributed by email to all the members in the district.

In 2005, the subject of complete retirement came up. Their decision was to retire to California.

"Well, Don retired," Nancy comments. "Wives don't retire."

Not to be overlooked in this prologue is another "personality" frequently mentioned in Nancy's articles. She is Missy, the Troyers' dog. In reality, Missy is two dogs.

"Missy Snow Star was our first Bichon (of the subgroup Havanese). She traveled with us from 1987 to 1998, when we had to put her to sleep because of seizures and congestive heart failure," Nancy says. "She was a sweet eight-pound ball of fur and was president of my fan club. She had bonded to me and followed me everywhere."

After Missy Snow Star, the Troyers acquired another Bichon, this one of the Bolognese subgroup. "Her official name is Oriana, but I labeled her Missy Moon Pie because she is such a clown. With the right trainer, she could leap tall buildings in a single bound," says Nancy.

When the Troyers moved to California, they settled at the Sun Lakes Country Club fifty-five-plus retirement community in Banning. How is "retirement" going? After reading Nancy's inspiring, emotional, and uplifting accounts that illustrate how much easier it is to navigate through life's challenges when you place implicit trust in God's promises, join us in the epilogue for an update.

Robert O. Vincent
Santa Paula, California
Spring 2011

Notes on . . .
Confronting Life's Challenges

Accidents	Disasters	Pain
Danger	Health Issues	Uncertainty
Death		

DEEP AND WIDE

*"Do you think you can explain the mystery of God? Do you think you
can diagram God Almighty? God is far higher than you can imagine, far
deeper than you can comprehend, stretching farther than earth's horizons,
far wider than the endless ocean."*　　　　　　—Job 11:7, The Message

I love the ocean. Its fresh salty air caresses my mind like my mother's lulla-
bies in the night. Whenever I visit my folks, I try to squeeze in a trip to the
beach because I just love being there—the sound of the waves, the comforting
feel of the sand sifting through my fingers or rubbing against my bare feet. What
bothers me about the sea is its size. In my childhood, I developed a fear when I
imagined huge tidal waves engulfing me. Even today, the fear faintly holds on to
my thoughts.

The day after Christmas in 2004, when most people on the planet were still
enjoying the holidays—we ourselves were vacationing on the Isle of Capri off Italy. The
sea had turned into a sinister beast on the other side of the globe.

I was in our hotel room packing my suitcase and wondering whether we
were going to make it off the island because even the Mediterranean Sea was
churning up white caps and most of the small tourist boats were grounded. We
tuned to CNN on television—our one link to the English-speaking world while
we were on our trip—and learned that earlier in the day, half a world away,
people were wading in the water or combing the beach for seashells or other treasures, when the tide receded farther than it ever had before. Many stood trans-
fixed by this oddity of nature, never suspecting something terrible was about to
happen. The horizon looked different, but people couldn't quite figure it out. All
at once, the biggest wave anyone had ever seen came crashing onto the shore. It
was a tsunami, or tidal wave, resulting from an underwater earthquake.

Before the waves abated, thousands of people were just plain gone and
hundreds of thousands were homeless. Most Americans couldn't comprehend
this natural disaster, even though late the previous year a series of hurricanes had
devastated Florida.

As we continued to listen, we learned that a place we knew—the white sands and azure blue waters off Phuket Island in Thailand—had been caught in this daytime nightmare. During the Vietnam era, we had lived in Thailand for two years and we knew the Thais to be a happy people who welcomed foreigners like us to share in the bounty of their country.

Returning to the task at hand of getting off the island and back on our trip, Stephanie made a quick call to our taxi friend to see if there was any possibility of getting on a boat to the mainland that day. He said we should hurry, so we soon were rolling our luggage up the street to the taxi stand. From there we were on the fast track, whizzing down the curving roads to the dock where we soon found ourselves standing on the top deck of an auto transport ship.

Halfway through the trip, I gave up my self-appointed guard duty for our luggage and joined Don and Steph on deck. The ship rolled as we watched the white caps on the angry waters. The power of the sea is good, but it reminded me of those lost in the tsunami and the thousands grieving for their families, homes, and very livelihood.

I asked myself an answerless question: "Why?"

Many of God's ways are a mystery, like the death of my younger brother Steve in the prime of his life. But one thing I know for sure—time is running out. The sea seems to mock my speculations with its endless boundaries, but I know that the God who created the sea and its power is also planning a rescue mission for all who come to Him through Jesus. He is mightier and deeper than the sea, but He also is more merciful than our own mothers and fathers. And His message to each of us is "Come, ye blessed of my Father, inherit the kingdom prepared for you from the foundation of the world" (Matthew 25:34).

RELEASING THE PAIN

And God shall wipe away all tears from their eyes; and there shall be no more death, neither sorrow, nor crying, neither there shall be any more pain: for the former things are passed away. —Revelation 21:4

I'm thankful for our pets, amid so many people, friends, and relatives in trouble healthwise:

My beloved Aunt M, when she was in the last stages of cancer.

My dear friend's brother—an energetic youth pastor—just being diagnosed with liver cancer.

And an old friend's wife, who is struggling to keep hopes alive for recovery from cancer because the caregivers are delaying treating her because it's considered a "small" cancer.

I look into my dog Missy's eyes and see such innocence and unconditional love and I gather her up in my arms and just hug her, feeling the warmth of her body and the soft, silky pile of her shorn tresses. I thank God that He gave her to me to be with me right now, to release some of the pain.

I wonder if Adam felt that way when he gathered up that first pure white lamb when he had to leave the Garden of Eden.

I thought that slaying that first sacrificial lamb was a sort of punishment for sinning. Yes, I know it was also a look into the future to give Adam and Eve a picture of the day when Jesus would stand in their place, suffering because of their sin, but I also wonder if, in this act of the first sacrifice, God placed that lamb in their arms to heal their deep grief of losing so much, to release some of the pain.

What a wonderful Savior!

A PIECE OF US

"Don't let this throw you. You trust God, don't you? Trust me. There is plenty of room for you in my Father's home. If that weren't so, would I have told you that I'm on my way to get a room ready for you? And if I'm on my way to get your room ready, I'll come back and get you so you can live where I live."
　　　　　　　　　　　　　　　　　　—John 14:1–3, The Message

As I watched her walk into the "ticket holders only" section of the airport, I thought back to the time, years ago in Germany, when we almost lost her.

It was a sunny summer afternoon in Herforst. The two of us were just returning to our apartment after feeding the vacationing neighbor's dog across the street. Suddenly, out of the corner of my eye to the left, I saw a tour bus descending on us gearing up to full throttle as it exited our quiet little town. I screamed out her name with all my might, "Stephanie!" and this usually independent little toddler turned her head toward me and froze in place just as the speeding bus zoomed by only inches from her little feet. It was so quick that it almost seemed unreal, except that we could still smell the exhaust in the churned-up air around us. I hugged Stephi tightly, thankful she was unhurt and realizing just how close I had come to losing her on that narrow village street.

That was years ago, but it was fresh in my memory because we were at the airport saying Goodbye to her as our little girl. Knowing we were standing in the middle of our emerging empty nest—parents without children (in residence, that is)—I thought of the day, many years before, when I took a flight out of San Diego and my parents said Goodbye to me as their little girl. I was joining my husband, Don, at Fort Benning, Georgia, to begin our new home. My parents still wanted to protect me, like any parents would, but the time had come to part. However, a piece of them went with me, just as a piece of us went with Stephi that week.

You know, I'm sure that's just the way Jesus feels—a piece of us goes with Him wherever we are.

At the Frankfurt Servicemen's Center, we had an art piece showing Jesus wearing a coat of many nations. A piece of every human being in history is draped around His everlasting shoulders. They, too, are His children, and He reaches out to you to show them that Jesus is real, and that unlike any other religion on the face of this earth, He loves them unconditionally. When they are cold in the fear and loneliness of these last days, He puts His coat of many promises around their shoulders, using your hands, because a piece of all of us is always in His heart.

REMEMBERING MY CLOSE CALLS

"Can a mother forget her nursing child? Can she feel no love for the child she has borne? But even if that were possible, I would not forget you! See, I have written your name on the palms of my hands." —Isaiah 49:15, 16a, NLT

It was late at night and my stomach was full of delicious Valentino's pizza. We were heading west out of Nebraska at Christmastime with piles of snow lining the highway. Mom was sitting to my right in the passenger seat and Don and our little schnauzer Fritzy were soundly asleep in the van bed in the back. The radio station faded as we sped down the highway headed for California. Then in short order, Mom, too, became silent in peaceful slumber.

Suddenly, without warning, I was startled by an awful sound as the emergency brake cables were ripped from the belly of the van. I got a firmer hold on the steering wheel just in time to avoid a major off-the-road incident. I was rather shaken up by that time and Don was wide awake, alerting me, as if I didn't know, that we had just had a close brush with death.

"Are you trying to kill us?" The rhetorical question was dismissed after we stopped and Don investigated the damage done by a highway reflector marker to the underside of his precious van. I knew full well I was supposed to remain alert, but the tires' rhythmic sounds and lack of radio or Mom talk just lulled me to sleep, almost permanently!

We drove on in silence—wide awake. We gulped as we passed a semi truck parked on the same area of the road where I had veered off just a mile earlier. I thought to myself, *Nancy, shame on you!* But there was a deeper meaning as we passed the exit to Ogallala, Nebraska. This was the same place my brother Steve and his bride Sharilyn had tried to enter the interstate just a few months previously when they had been hit by a truck and killed.

That night, we stopped at a gas station and plugged in our heater, but couldn't sleep. We had come so close to hitting that semi just a short distance farther down the road, and so close to repeating the tragic death of my brother and his wife.

I opened my Sabbath School lesson to find something to comfort me, and as I glanced at the subject, I couldn't believe my eyes. It was titled "Saved to Serve." Gratefully, I bowed my head in a prayer of thanksgiving for God's protection for all four of us. I shuddered to think what sadness would have enveloped our families if that close call had turned into a fatal accident. Just then in the midst of these somber thoughts, I remembered a favorite song:

"When I'm worried and I can't sleep, I count my blessings instead sheep and I fall asleep, counting my blessings."[1]

Right there in the deep of night, I counted my blessings, one by one. I plan one day to write a book titled, *Counting My Close Calls.* I think God has blessed me with enough vagabond experiences to fill a book. I know I will be blessed by it because one thing I know for sure—there have been many more close calls than I really have been aware of.

That goes for you too. When you get down, when you feel that God is on vacation and you aren't really that important, count your close calls and your blessings.

God is good. He loves to hold you in the palm of His hand. And above all, whether we are spared or not from some future tragedy, God still promises that He will never forget us.

That's God for you—always blessing, always there, ready for that grand homecoming.

"Heavenly Father, open my eyes."

TAXI ANGEL

It is a good thing to give thanks unto the Lord, and to sing praises unto thy name, O Most High: To shew forth thy lovingkindness in the morning, and thy faithfulness every night. —Psalm 92:1, 2

It was a Sunday morning in 1995, less than a week until the end of Don's one-year assignment as an army chaplain at Camp Howze, a remote post thirty miles north of Seoul, not far from the border between North and South Korea.

I quickly rinsed off the breakfast dishes and called Stephi to come along. We were going to drive to Camp Howze with a backseat full of personal items we were taking to Don for a last mailing to the United States.

I had had a very busy year as director of the International Servicemen's Center located on the Korean Union Adventist Compound, but we had made such good friends, and I learned to cook for big crowds.

We turned right, leaving the parking lot to get into a mass of traffic that ran like overflowing rivers in every direction. As we neared the main train station, I could see out of the corner of my eye something moving. I quickly moved to the middle of the road to avoid it, but it kept coming so I took the unprecedented step of moving across the double line to get out of the way. When I realized that wasn't going to work, I moved back to the right side of the road when I heard the most awful sound—a kind of a thud. Cold chills ran down my spine as I quickly moved off the road onto the shoulder, which in Korea is known as the sidewalk.

I stopped and turned to my daughter and said, "My life is over as I know it, Stephi! I just hit someone!"

I got out of the car and went quickly to the man lying crumpled on the street. "Are you all right?" I asked, wondering how he could even move after such an impact. He muttered something in Korean. He had the unmistakable smell of liquor on his breath. I figured he must have tried to run across the street in an alcoholic stupor.

Just then a police officer rushed over and asked me to get back in my car with Stephi and make a U-turn. I could hear the siren of an ambulance that was coming to the scene. We drove up the street to a small medical clinic. The policeman asked me to park and go inside.

I found a seat in the middle of a mass of mostly empty metal chairs. Behind me and over to the left sat one other individual. Soon the ambulance personnel hurried the man into the clinic on a gurney.

As I sat rocking myself in nervous anxiety, twelve-year-old Stephi walked calmly to the pay telephone and called her physical education teacher at the Adventist elementary school. The teacher was our best hope in this situation. He spoke fluent Korean, even though he was from Australia.

The rumors we had heard from other wives who had sworn they would never drive in Seoul were pretty scary. The story was that Americans always were the ones found at fault in such accidents and would be punished. I rocked some more as I prepared to accept the fact that my future fate could include being locked up in a Korean jail.

Soon Stephi's teacher arrived. He was smiling and held out his hand. "You are very lucky," he said. "Did you notice that man behind you?" I mumbled a "No," feeling anything but social at the moment.

"Well," the teacher said, "he testified on your behalf. He is a taxi driver and was parked at the crosswalk when the man came out and ran into your car. He said the light was red for pedestrians and that you had the right of way."

I smiled over my shoulder at the stranger-now-my-hero. "There's more," the teacher went on. "The taxi driver is an Adventist." I slumped back in my chair, still concerned about the drunken pedestrian. "Don't worry," the teacher said. "They'll fix him up."

I hugged the teacher and then the taxi driver, and before leaving talked to the police officer, who asked me to visit the precinct later in the week to take care of the paperwork. Then with a wry smile, he asked me as he was leaving my car, "Are you related to Jimmy Carter? You look like you could be his sister." I chuckled inwardly at the question and was surprised that the Korean officer could speak such good English.

Former President Carter had been in Korea a short time earlier for a peace conference between North and South Korea. The Koreans loved him for his help, and remotely I was benefitting from his popularity.

I breathed a prayer of gratitude as Stephi and I continued toward our original destination. Don's chapel at Camp Howze was still an hour's drive away. I knew I had to get back and drive the car right away or I wouldn't drive another mile in Korea, and we had a lot of errands to run before our flight back to the United States in five days.

By the time we arrived at Camp Howze I had relaxed a bit. Don wondered where we had been and I told him the story about the guardian angel in the taxi who went against traditional nationalism to testify on my behalf.

Notes on . . . Confronting Life's Challenges | 21

Sometimes I sing an old Irving Berlin song to remind me: "When I'm worried and I can't sleep, I count my blessings [my close calls] instead of sheep, and I fall asleep, counting my blessings." This indeed was one of my "close calls" and I was counting them then as I still do today. It has been years since we left Korea, and finally I can type this story without breaking out in a cold sweat.

I know I was blessed. Even when I had no idea what the future held, God placed a fellow believer with a conscience exactly where and when I would need him most. And that was just one of the instances I knew about. How many other miracles have there been that you or I never recognize? Indeed, it is good to praise the Lord. It is good to thank Him for His loving kindness!

ONLY GOD KNOWS

"I will lead the blind by ways they have not known, along unfamiliar paths I will guide them; I will turn the darkness into light before them and make the rough places smooth. These are the things I will do; I will not forsake them." —Isaiah 42:16, NIV

I slipped behind the steering wheel of our RV to give Don a rest from driving. We had traveled quite a distance and were now on the streets of a town in Virginia with just a few hours to go before we would be safely home.

Don had gone into the bathroom and was out of earshot. Suddenly, ahead, I saw a woman on the sidewalk striking a man. I watched in disbelief as the couple's fight intensified from hand-hitting to wide swings with the woman's purse.

Then without warning, the couple stepped out into traffic directly in front of my moving motor home. I quickly stepped on the brakes to avoid hitting them. Then I heard a muffled objection of some sort from the back of the RV and a door flew open.

"What are you doing?" Don shouted. He hadn't seen the couple fighting so he thought I was driving erratically. All he knew was that I had stopped the vehicle, causing him to crash through the shower door in a most objectionable manner.

I tried to explain the situation, asking our daughter Stephi to vouch for my story because by that time the couple was nowhere in sight. She chimed in, acknowledging that she had seen the couple fighting too. Gently I tried to convince Don that I had not planned his demise but only reacted to an emergency situation.

Yes, it was true, occasionally when things had become boring on long trips like this, one of us would play a prank or two on the other to lighten the moment. However, this time that wasn't the case. How I wished Don had seen what I saw.

Sometimes I question why God stops me in midstream—why He puts on the brakes, so to speak, when I'm sure I know what is best for me. I don't see what my heavenly Father sees because I have stepped into the water closet of my fears, thus losing His perspective.

"Lord Jesus, help me trust You through the hills and valleys of my life. Forgive me for my unbelief in the ultimate goodness of Your will. Open my heart to receive what only You know to be best for my life. Open my eyes. Amen!"

HAND SIGNALS

> *Behold, I have engraved you on the palms of my hands.*
> —Isaiah 49:16, ESV

I was extremely upset as I stepped out of my car and evaluated the damage done by a large semi truck parked just ahead of me. I was in the right, I thought, driving up on the right side of a truck that didn't seem to be up to anything unusual. But I was wrong. I hadn't seen the red blinking turn signals as I cruised along beside the truck. Suddenly, I was horrified as the truck entered my lane. I heard the sound of crunching metal. Shocked, I yelled. I was mad. What was he doing? And finally the trucker stopped.

When police officers arrived, the trucker explained his side of the story. He had been turning right on a wide angle to avoid the curb. He had activated his turn signals, too, and here was this teenager . . . I objected with a bit of mildly suppressed hysteria. "Wait a minute, sir. You didn't use your turn signal!" It was then that we both realized what had happened. He hadn't seen me beside him because I was located in his blind spot and I hadn't seen his signal because I was beside him, not behind him.

There were no cell phones then but somehow I got to a nearby phone and called my father. "Dad," I said between sobs, "I've been in an accident. I'm so sorry!" There was a pause and then Dad replied with just the right words that I needed so desperately at that moment. After all, this was Dad's car we were talking about. He asked, "Are you all right?" That question took me aback for a moment. "Well, yes, I'm OK . . ."

Suddenly there was a big space in my heart with a question mark. Was I OK? My thoughts wandered off briefly to memories of accidents I had driven by in the past. Then I came back to the present situation. "But Dad, what about your car?" I offered, timidly. He assured me he was far more interested in my well-being than the condition of the car. It was then that I settled back in a cushion of care enveloped in my father's love.

To this day, that's all I remember—no details about the car or the cost of repair or the police report. The instant my dad responded so lovingly to his errant daughter's actions, that memory became a proverb and turned my thoughts toward my heavenly Father, who doesn't use blinkers at all to communicate with me when I mess up. He uses hand signals. "Nancy," He says, "are you OK? You know I love you. Just look at My hands."

HOW DO YOU . . . ?

> *And now, dear brothers and sisters, we want you to know what will*

happen to the believers who have died so you will not grieve like people
who have no hope. —*1 Thessalonians 4:13, NLT*

Christmas 1963: I was home for the holidays from Pacific Union College.
The previous month President Kennedy had been assassinated and it seemed our
world had turned upside down.

Before sunrise on Christmas Day, our family received a call that my grandmother had died during the night. Grandma, a stately German lady in her sixties
who lived in Lodi, California, had been cleaning up after one of her famous
family reunions. We didn't expect her to be gone so soon.

I remember playing a Chipmunks' Christmas album but the tunes still didn't
lighten my heart. Later, I sat alone in a park across the street pondering life,
death, and heaven at the young age of eighteen.

On another December day a few years ago, we received a phone call that
brought great sadness and turned our hearts toward home. Our church conference president, Dave Cress; conference secretary, Jim Frost; new assistant to the
president, Clay Farwell; and our communications secretary, Jamie Amall, and a
pilot, had died in a plane crash. Again Christmas lights and tunes became hollow.

In 1963, I saved an article titled "Peace on Earth" clipped from the *Inglewood Daily News* that blessed and healed my heart. I pass it along with the prayer
that it will heal your hearts and turn them toward home:

> How do you say "Merry Christmas" to someone who has lost a
> beloved father, husband, friend? How do you say "Merry Christmas" to
> someone forced out of old and dear familiar surroundings? How do you
> say "Merry Christmas" to someone cringing with pain or dulled by illness?
> You don't exactly. You reach, instead, back through the long years to
> a small village to a tiny child—a child born to suffer, born to die, born to
> give love and life and hope to all the world; a child born to teach us how
> to be men and women, how to be human and humane, how to worship
> our Creator by living our faith; born that we might forever, through the
> centuries and the generations, have the happiness that comes only from
> surrendering ourselves to the One who made us; that we might know
> the solace of releasing what we can't keep forever, and the joy of remem-
> bering what no grief, no pain can make us ever forget. You reach back;
> and if you reach far enough, to a silent holy night, you hear the words
> that can be said to anyone, anytime—words that are a prayer and a bene-
> diction; words that encompass the hopes of all who suffer or sorrow, the
> hopes of all men of good will: "Peace on Earth."

We don't grieve as others without faith, but we do miss these precious ministers of the gospel of Jesus Christ. Each one was special to many of us and their
absence will remind us that we have a blessed hope in Jesus, our Friend and
Savior, who is preparing a home for us in heaven.

Notes on . . .
Making the Right Choices

Participate or Refrain	*Self or Others*
Speak or Be Silent	*Sacred or Secular*
Act or Be Patient	*Help or Pass On By*

FOOTPRINTS IN THE SNOW

I saw her in the Base Exchange—Lucy, a sweet young mother-to-be. She was expecting her first baby, and though her face was pale from the trials of pregnancy, I could see the expectant joy glowing from her face. She had expectations, I certainly realized that, especially as she patted her emerging tummy saying that even though relatives thought she should be bigger at six months, her doctor said she was right on schedule.

Later that same day, I was walking through the snow and looked back over my shoulder to see one set of footprints in the snow—mine! The landscape had been so pristine, so perfectly flawless before I had walked on it. In a way, I wished that everyone would just stay at home and keep it that way. These weren't my expectations, however—just silly thoughts. I knew very well why the footprints irritated me. That same day my Christianity had been tested.

A couple had come for help, and although I had helped them, I knew I could have done so much more. I was ashamed, and through the night I chastised myself through tears, really expecting more from myself. I wished I could retrace my steps and leave the scene as pure as God had made it. I wished I could turn back the clock, but no one can retrace his or her steps, not really.

We can move ahead walking in His steps, taking time to let Him feed our souls and transform our hearts to be like Jesus. We can't do it. Really, no matter how virtuous we see ourselves, we really aren't pure as the driven snow.

That is the first part of the gospel. The second half helps me sleep at night, especially when it's snowing. Jesus, the Son of God, our Savior, our blood Brother, wants to carry us through the snow and the only set of footprints in the snow will be His! Sing this prayer song along with me:

"I want, Dear Lord, a heart that's pure and clean,
A sunlit heart without a cloud between,
A heart like Thine, a heart divine, a heart that's white as snow.
On me, Dear Lord, a heart like this bestow."[2]

TAP ME ON THE SHOULDER

But the Comforter . . . whom the Father will send in my name, he shall teach you all things, and bring all things to your remembrance. —John 14:26

I was watching the clouds rush by on my trip to Bangkok when my thoughts turned to my grandparents who lived in Santa Rosa, California, where I had just left.

Earlier that day, I had combed my grandma's hair. She wasn't that old or dying or anything but she asked me to brush her hair before I left for my plane. It was a simple request but unusual for Grandma and me. As I let the comb run through her dark, curly hair, I saw her differently. She seemed a bit vulnerable and I sensed she was letting me know how much she loved me.

I probably would have forgotten that event except that before our two years abroad were completed, Grandma died. I didn't get the chance to comfort her because I was living so far away. Nor did I get to hug Grandpa or Aunt M and tell them what a blessing Grandma had been.

Later, when we were going through Grandma's things, I found a poem she had written just for me. I also found readings such as "Waiting for the Train" that Grandma had given at large gatherings. Since I also enjoy performing, I felt a special kinship with her. Still, the poem is what I treasure most.

As I looked through her things, I became homesick for days gone by, wishing I could go back and ask both my grandparents questions such as what it was like to live during the Depression. Grandma's maiden name was Service and she was related to the great storyteller Robert Service, but we never talked about that. I wish we had. There were so many experiences I wanted to relive.

Unfortunately, I never concentrated on my grandparents long enough to really learn what was in their hearts. They lived just a bus ride away from the college, yet I didn't go there very often. I was young and occupied with my own life at college. In retrospect, I am sorry that I didn't have a bigger heart, a wider vision, and a sense of what a treasure they really were.

I have begun to understand that the true superstars of this life don't have their names on theater marquees or CD covers. They often are right next to us on park benches, doctor's office sofas, in supermarket checkout lines, and even in church pews, and they could share valuable lessons.

There is One unseen Guest who knows what my grandparents must have felt—that they were being taken for granted. A scene in the Christian classic *My Heart Christ's Home* depicts Jesus patiently sitting on the sofa in the living room of my heart, just waiting to talk. How many times have I passed by that door, too busy, too occupied with things instead of people?

Dear heavenly Father, tap me on the shoulder, teach me Your will, bring to mind those lessons You have given me today, in the precious name of Jesus, Amen.

GLORY RIDE

Now unto him that is able to keep you from falling, and to present you

faultless before the presence of his glory with exceeding joy, to the only
wise God our Saviour, be glory and majesty, dominion and power, both
now and ever. Amen. —Jude 1:24, 25

Trees rushed by as we made our way toward Athens, Georgia, and the last event on our schedule. Visits to the doctor and errands had kept us on the road for all of that long, hot day.

We rounded the corner to the parking lot to find a couple of familiar cars waiting. Laughter filled the air as we greeted one another. Silently I sent up a prayer of thanksgiving for these friends who had taken the time to come out.

It was cool and quiet as we entered the sanctuary. Our study was the book of Jude, written by Jesus' brother. But before we began, Don asked for any prayer requests. Without hesitation, many of those in attendance shared various needs and concerns, each one reflecting tenderness and longing for miracles for grandmothers, friends, coworkers, and relatives.

It was good to relax and share with friends. Then the doors opened and a short, bearded man carrying a couple of grocery sacks quickly found a seat near the back. Don closed the study as we sang a benediction song from the book of Jude—the one you see above.

It seemed the evening was over but Kathy stood up and asked to share something. She pulled out a beautiful handmade yellow shawl, putting it around my shoulders. Tears began to well up because I knew how precious this gift was. It was a prayer shawl handmade by Kathy during the prayer shawl ministry, to bless me. I ran my fingers through the soft homespun weave of triple stitches representing the loving care of the Trinity.

Meanwhile, the bearded man was beginning to mumble some kind of complaint from the back row. He said he hadn't been in this church before but wondered if some of us knew him. His words seemed pressed together and confusing and I was growing a little irritated that he was there.

Guilty thoughts also seemed to invade my peace and comfort as I realized how precious this man was to God. Finally, we all made our way outside, checking occasionally on Don who had decided to talk to the man alone.

We chatted nervously, wondering when the night would be over. Soon Don helped the man out the door and into our car. *Oh,* I thought nervously, *is this wise?* But before I could ponder that thought for very long, we were on our way. Now the bearded man who was sitting in the seat behind me had a name— Aaron. He asked me what I thought of what he was talking about and I offered that he was talking a bit too fast for me to understand him. That was a mistake because Aaron didn't appreciate the remark. The bearded man in the backseat was now an offended backseat driver.

We finally arrived where Aaron had asked to go and as he opened the car door, we parted with a blessing. As we turned to go home, we saw Aaron walking briskly on the overpass toward the hotel where he said he was staying. I had been strangely blessed by so many things that day—friends, doctors, salesmen, and even Aaron, the bearded man.

Questions peppered my guilty soul like sleet. *Had I shown Jesus' love to Aaron?* Now exhausted from so many concerns of the day, I pictured in my mind what it will be like to stand right in the center of God's love. Beams of yellow sunshine will stream from my heavenly Father, ever waiting for me to ask for a full measure of His mercy. But I don't stand there alone. The arms of Jesus Christ surround me, just as Don had described that evening.

This is no joyride of my imagination but a glory ride for eternity. Thank You, Jesus!

ABOVE ALL THINGS

> *There is a way that seems right to a man, but in the end it leads to death.*
> —*Proverbs 16:25, NIV*

The rain was coming down in torrents as I drove through several small towns on my way home from prayer meeting. Between those cute little communities, the street lights disappeared, making it difficult to see little more than the road directly ahead. Off to the right, huge flood lights appeared as a train approached, blinding me further. I certainly would be glad to get home!

Thankfully, the road ahead was straight, so I drove on, recalling in my mind conversations from earlier that evening. I smiled as I thought of the sweet folk who had braved the elements to come out and study the Bible. There had been a sweet spirit around that table as we shared God's Word. At the end of the meeting, the phone rang and we learned of an answered prayer from another church member who hadn't been able to come, but who just wanted to share her good news. What a perfect way to end prayer meeting!

My thoughts returned to the road ahead as I saw the airport sign indicating my turnoff. Just then, I noticed that the caution bars were down and the red lights were flashing.

I would have to wait this one out, I thought, but I was in no hurry. The train would be by shortly. Other cars appeared on the opposite side of the tracks, their headlights glaring into my front window.

Boy, it was dark, I thought to myself. The minutes ticked by and I noticed some cars turning around and disappearing into the night. Then suddenly, I watched in disbelief as several cars on the other side of the tracks zigzagged between the warning bars and crossed the railroad passing by my car.

I pondered my next move. Should I do that too? I summed up the situation:
1. A very dark night.
2. Too much pouring rain.
3. Definitely low visibility.
4. The possibility of a speeding train like one I had seen a month before.

I decided not to follow the crowd. Sure, it was late, but I had no desire to put myself in harm's way. By the time I could see the train, I reasoned, with my luck it would be right on top of me. So I turned around and left the cars behind me to make their own decisions.

As I drove down the road toward the middle of town, I thought of those crazy people who had decided to cross the tracks. I wasn't that much different from them. Many times I had made this or that decision carelessly without really thinking.

I remembered a verse from the night's study: "But the end of all things is at hand; therefore be serious and watchful in your prayers. And above all things have fervent love for one another, for 'love will cover a multitude of sins' "
(1 Peter 4:7, 8, NKJV).

"Dear Lord," I prayed, "if it is Your will, let me live another day to share Your love with those You put in my path. Amen."

EXCHANGING PASSIONS

To this you were called, because Christ suffered for you, leaving you an example, that you should follow in his steps. —1 Peter 2:21, NIV

I stepped off the bus in San Francisco, eager to get back to my college situated above California's beautiful Napa Valley. I had just one more bus connection to make and then I would be back at school with my friends.

Having an extra long layover, I wandered around the bus terminal looking for something to occupy my time. "That's what I need," I muttered to myself, "a good book to read!"

My eyes scanned the many brightly colored paperbacks on the shelves and I was drawn to a racy title. Quickly I moved to the counter to purchase it before climbing back onto the bus to begin reading the gripping romance novel. It drew me in with its easy-to-read style and descriptions of emotions I could only imagine.

Before I knew it, I was hooked. I began seeking books to feed my growing appetite. As I look back analyzing my obsession, my conscience seemed to be in a daze. I heard no little voice telling me to stop. How could this be? I was a leader at my Christian college—why did I read that stuff? My mind neither answered nor asked the question.

The school year finally ended and I was back home for summer vacation. One day, I searched the shelves for interesting books when I spotted one with a black cover in the middle of all the colorful ones. I reached up to get the hardcover volume and as I brought it down to eye level and opened it, time seemed to stand still.

I began to read the story of a city preacher and his surprised congregation. I quickly found myself drawn in to read a completely different kind of novel,

Charles Sheldon's *In His Steps*. I couldn't put the book down, not even long enough to wipe the tears welling up in my eyes. I felt freedom sweep over me like a beautiful waterfall and when I came up for air, I could breathe again. I laughed as I began to realize that I was free.

For months I read and reread the story of a church changed by one simple question: "What would Jesus do?" My addiction to sordid novels immediately became a thing of the past. Reading *In His Steps* changed the direction of my life. By God's grace and intervention (Thank you, Lord!), I turned my attention from the passions of this world to the passions of Paradise.

A SAFE PLACE

It will be a shelter and shade from the heat of the day, and a refuge and hiding place from the storm and rain. —Isaiah 4:6, NIV

It was Saturday night and Don and I eagerly jumped out of the car and headed for the nearby restaurant. This was going to be a great night. Our friend Charles was the main entertainment. We sat in front of the stage to enjoy the performance as Charles crooned out song after song in his unforgettable mellow style.

After a few sodas, I was heading for the restroom when suddenly a well-dressed man approached me. "Could you give me a hug?" he said warmly. Without a thought in my head, I replied, "Sure!" I gave him one of my leftover church hugs from earlier that day, figuring he must know me.

To my embarrassment, he hugged me back—in a nonchurch style. I was taken aback and lowered my head as I made a beeline for my original destination.

Stephi was close behind and asked me what was going on. I was confused and angry at myself at the same time. What was I thinking? This wasn't church! Finally, I got up enough courage to rejoin our friends who were still listening to the music, passing the spot where the stranger had approached me. He called out something friendly from a far corner. I looked the other way and quickly found a safe spot surrounded by my friends.

During a break in the entertainment, I told the rest of my family and friends what had happened. They laughed heartily, thinking it funny that I would be so naïve as to give out one of my church hugs to a total stranger in a restaurant. I was embarrassed and again chided myself silently for my stupidity. *Nancy, you don't give just anyone a hug. This isn't church!*

The next Sabbath at church during the welcoming portion of the service, everyone stood and freely greeted friends and strangers alike all around the sanctuary. I joined in the hugs and smiles and handshakes with a bit of relief in my heart. This is where I could hug folk freely without being misunderstood. This is where God lives—a sort of refuge from the outside world and its strange preoccupations.

When we were seated again, I relaxed in my pew, thanking God that I had this opportunity to reach out to others in the name of Jesus without any fear for myself. It was good to be a part of the family of God, to be able to tell people "Happy Sabbath" or "You are loved!" or "I'm so glad you came today!"

These holy hugs were little bits of heaven, a glimpse of the future where we will walk safely side by side with Jesus and all those who love Him.

As I left church that day and every Sabbath since, I often look back at those special gathering places and smile deep down in my ever-learning heart. His house, indeed, is a safe place!

NO CRACKS FOR ME, LORD

So humble yourselves under the mighty power of God, and at the right time he will lift you up in honor. Give all your worries and cares to God, for he cares about you. —1 Peter 5:6, 7, NLT

When troubles come your way, consider it an opportunity for great joy. —James 1:2, NLT

I turned around and let my eyes follow the sounds from the back of the RV. I could see a flurry of activity back where our then nine-year-old daughter Stephanie was apparently jumping on the bed. She was bouncing evasively, punching the air, dropping to her knees, tumbling off the bed over and over again.

Finally, my curiosity caused me to slip out my comfortable front seat and make my way back to where she was. "Stephanie Dawn Troyer!" I called out in mock irritation, "What are you doing?" Without stopping, Stephi replied between gasps, "I'm 'rasslin' with Hobbes, Mom!" Stephi loved reading about the adventures of Calvin and Hobbes—philosophical cartoon stories about a boy and his tiger.

I walked back up the motor home aisle and collapsed in laughter. "Well," Don asked, "What's Stephi up to now?" I explained the scene and he just chuckled to himself. "What a kid!"

Remembering that scene of long ago recently took me to the Calvin and Hobbes Web site on the Internet. One cartoon panel especially caught my attention.

Calvin is standing on a square of sidewalk with Hobbes nearby. He says, "Let's say life is like this square in the sidewalk. We're born at this crack and die at that crack . . . we find ourselves somewhere inside the square in the process of walking out of it. Suddenly we find our time in here is fleeting. Is our quick experience here pointless? Have we made the most of these precious few footsteps?" Calvin and Hobbes stand motionless as the sky grows darker.

I thought of my life between the cracks. How many hours have I spent 'rasslin' with my fears? Had I forgotten? Had I not heard that God has given me a secret weapon to fight the unseen enemy of my peace? The weapon is thanksgiving and its mission is healing.

I don't need to stand motionless in the darkness like Calvin and Hobbes.

This is what I hear Jesus saying to me: *"Step off the sidewalk of your fears, Nancy. Take hold of My Spirit of joy and rise above the little world of sidewalks!"*

"OK," I reply eagerly, "no cracks for me, Lord!"

LEST WE FORGET

"You have the keys, Nancy!" Don's urgent words brought me back to reality. There we stood in the sunny commissary parking lot, a bag boy waiting patiently as I tried to locate my car keys. Where were they?

I mentally retraced my steps trying to remember where I might have left the little suckers. Then I returned to the commissary and began the big FBI hunt for my keys. I grilled the cashier, emptied my purse, tossed all the lettuce from its bin, and pawed my way through Linda McCartney's newly discovered vegetarian cuisine—nothing. Absolutely no keys!

"They must be here!" I chastised myself. "Why had I let those keys dangle from my finger?" It was convenient then, sure. But now it wasn't. My groceries were defrosting in the parking lot! Finally, with every corner of the commissary searched, I gave up and headed home alone, driving the other car which had been brought to rescue me in my distress.

Sometimes I have been accused of looking mindless by my kin, when actually I had been deep in thought—creative thought, of course. Was I in the first stages of Alzheimer's? I really used to fear that I was in the first stages of that tragic disease, which I had seen slowly destroying so many bright, intelligent friends. But I had chased that fear away with the notion that if I did acquire it, I would be the last to know!

Seriously, I do feel sad for those family members who must carry all the pain of watching their loved ones who no longer remember even their names mentally waste away. But you know, there is another even more debilitating disease that threatens all of us, even those who can find their keys!

It is a tragic thing that we tend to forget how the Lord has lifted us up and protected us. If we forget, LEST we forget, we are as empty and powerless as those who carry Alzheimer's in their brains. The difference is that we have a choice, they don't!

We have a choice to dwell on the things of God that are life-saving or to dwell on the negative stuff we find everywhere. "Whatsoever things are lovely, whatsoever things are pure, whatsoever things are of good report, if there be any virtue, if there be any praise, think on these things!"

You probably still want to know if I ever found my keys. Yes, I did! (This will preach too). I found them in a bag of grapes.

THE SNAKE PATH

For God so loved the world, that he gave his only begotten Son, that

whosoever believeth in him should not perish, but have everlasting life.
—*John 3:16*

With my arms stretched wide, I ran down the mountain path with a strange new freedom welling up inside. Moments earlier, I had been part of a tour group visiting Masada, a cliff-edged mountain plateau rising majestically above the Judean Desert south of Jerusalem.

The warm winds whipped my face as our tour guide told of courageous people who defied the Tenth Roman Legion for seven months after the fall of Jerusalem in A.D. 70. No enemy could attack without being spotted and there was ample food and water for the more than six hundred inhabitants.

Eventually, the Romans figured out a way to reach the top. They used prisoners of war to build a ramp to reach the gates. When the Romans broke down the walls of the fortress, they were met by an eerie silence. Everyone was found lying dead on the ground. They had chosen to escape by taking their own lives in preference to becoming Roman slaves. The hushed minority had found victory in death, the ultimate insult to the merciless Romans who knew how much they treasured life and freedom.

After we heard this remarkable story, we were shown the Snake Path leading to the valley. A zigzag pattern decorated the slope like one big Zorro brand. We had come up by cable car but I asked our guide how long it would take to go down on foot by way of the Snake Path. He said someone who really hurried probably could make it down to the bus in time.

I smiled at Don and he playfully replied, "You can't do that!" That was all the challenge I needed. For some reason, I just felt I had to do something after hearing of the courage of those who died rather than face captivity by the Romans.

Without another word, I slung my purse onto my back and headed down the path. Once, when I looked back, I saw the cable car starting to move and I continued my descent, turning and running and braking for what seemed like hours. I felt I should be at the bottom by now when I realized I was only halfway there. I continued the lonely race, trusting gravity to be in my favor. Finally, I saw the bus. My legs felt like spaghetti.

The Judean sun was beating down almost as mercilessly as the Roman siege on the ancient fortress. Don held me up as I made my last steps to the bus. My calf muscles felt paralyzed, but inside, deep down in my Masada heart, I felt like an Olympian using the last ounce of strength to make it over the finish line.

As I looked over my shoulder one last time at the lofty mountain refuge, I thought of those who had chosen death over slavery. Then I thought of that Friday in Jerusalem, centuries earlier just a few miles up the same dusty desert road, when Jesus of Nazareth took my place on a Roman cross. He chose to die for me so that I could choose to live for Him. Best of all, unlike those six hundred residents of Masada, He did not remain silent in the grave but rose to share the victory of the Resurrection!

NO SHORTCUTS

> *But those who wait for the Lord [who expect, look for, and hope in Him]*
> *shall change and renew their strength and power; they shall lift their wings*
> *and mount up [close to God] as eagles [mount up to the sun]; they shall*
> *run and not be weary, they shall walk and not faint or become tired.*
> —*Isaiah 40:31, AMP*

"Ha!" I laughed out loud at my little dog. "So you won't settle for the cheap way out!" Even though I had held the back door wide open, Missy sat glued to the top of the lounge chair. She was holding out for something better—a walk in the neighborhood with me!

A few moments earlier, I had been sitting on the side of my bed putting on my socks and Missy had been jumping up and down with anticipation. She seemed sure that a morning walk was just around the corner.

But as it too often happens, I got sidetracked and in my haste to get several things done at once, I had opened the door to let Missy out while I fixed breakfast.

When Missy would have nothing to do with that, I realized that my little twelve-pound dog was wiser than I was. She preferred to wait and walk with her master than to go out on her own.

Isaiah penned it well: "They that wait upon the Lord shall renew their strength."

"Dear Lord," I earnestly prayed, "help me to remember not to settle for the fast way out but to walk with You each morning. No backdoor shortcuts for me!"

PASS IT ON

> *O God, you are my God, earnestly I seek you; my soul thirsts for you, my*
> *body longs for you, in a dry and weary land where there is no water. I*
> *have seen you in the sanctuary and beheld your power and your glory.*
> *Because your love is better than life, my lips will glorify you. I will praise*
> *you as long as I live, and in your name I will lift up my hands.*
> —*Psalm 63:1–4, NIV*

I would like to share a parable.

Many years ago, there was a very young and thin pastor's wife we shall call Polly Doodle. After twelve moons of seminary studies, the pastor and Polly took a working holiday to a flaky Michigan town for a summer evangelistic series with a truckload of fellow seminarians.

One day, Polly was taken aside by another pastor's wife and asked to deliver a message of rebuke to a third pastor's wife. Having no personal feelings for the situation, yet feeling (mistakenly) wise, Polly went to the lady and delivered the message as kindly as she could that someone was requesting that the mother not feed her baby in public the natural way.

What happened next still holds a bit of mystery for the young and thin pastor's wife named Polly Doodle, for the mother turned quickly toward her and looked her squarely in the eyes. "Oh, come on, Polly. You don't have to beat around the bush. I know you are the one offended."

Polly did everything she could do to change the mother's opinion but nothing worked, so she let it go, chalking it up to "a lesson learned." Polly Doodle did not take kindly to becoming the middle woman and she vowed never again to pass on another's concern she did not share.

Polly's dilemma is one that many of us have experienced and it almost makes one want to cease any type of sharing. But there is something special here to remember because the good news of all good news is that there is one message that is always safe to pass on no matter where it puts you. It's the message of God's unconditional love—He loves you, no matter what. He will always love you!

This reminds me of a song I used to sing at summer camp titled "Pass It On."[3]

"It only takes a spark to get a fire going,
And soon all those around can warm up in its glowing.
That's how it is with God's love;
Once you've experienced it,
You spread His love to everyone;
You want to pass it on."

WALKING SHOES

Even though I walk through the valley of the shadow of death, I will fear no evil, for you are with me.   —*Psalm 23:4, NIV*

I stepped off the train in Frankfurt at the end of a rail adventure and took a closer look at my traveling companions. I'm not referring to my family, as precious as they are, but my super shoes—my Dansko clogs.

When I packed my suitcase in Georgia, I put in an extra pair of shoes just in case my heavy clogs wore me down, but that never happened. For twenty-one straight days, I wore them everywhere, except to bed. They kept my feet warm and protected, and it was easy to walk on any kind of road, especially the cobblestone streets in Europe. I'm sure I walked more in those three weeks than I walked all together in the previous year, and yet my feet did not hurt, were not bruised, and were ready to go again—almost.

I used to take my little dog Missy on walks every morning. It was good for her and good for me. I needed to build up stamina since my shoulder surgery and she needed and liked the exercise too. So off to walk we would go. But since returning home, I have found it more difficult to keep that appointment. At first, when the weather was warm, I took her every day and she was so happy. For some reason, walking with me was more fun for my Missy than her forbidden roaming of our neighborhood. Why haven't I done it lately? Simply, it's cold outside! Bad excuse, you say? You are right. "Cold outside" is NO excuse!

When I recall the many walks I have taken, it seems I've walked all over creation in my many years. Yet the walks of the past really don't matter now. My favorite book is *Walk Across America*. I've always had a fantasy that I would just walk down a road and keep walking—or up a mountain until I reached the top. But walking with my fingers on the computer keys as I'm doing right now really doesn't count for good health. So what shall I do? Should I take a trip to a mountain and walk there? Or should I try the road right here at home? We all know the answer to that one and it's said beautifully in a phrase you've heard before, "Bloom where you are planted."

I'm thinking the same about my spiritual life—my time with Jesus. Should I read about others' walk with God? As good as that is, will that count? Or should I make a reservation for a women's retreat and talk to Him when I get there? Or as the gardener's maxim says, should I just walk where I am?

I think I'll start right here, right now, walking in the neighborhood, praying for the neighborhood, talking to my Savior about the big things and the little things—my worries, my anxieties, my joys, and the taste of food on my tongue, perhaps. That sounds silly but really it isn't, because talking to Jesus about anything is talking to Jesus about us—the Creator of the universe and me.

I hereby leave the computer chair to take time to face the present by walking out the door and down the street where I belong. That's a present to me, don't you think?

HEAVY SHOES

They that wait upon the LORD shall renew their strength; they shall mount up with wings as eagles; they shall run, and not be weary; they shall walk, and not faint. —*Isaiah 40:31*

The phones had stopped ringing and there was a lull in the day's activities when I spotted Bob, waiting silently in his blue work uniform near the entrance. I sauntered over to him, expecting an exchange of some small pleasantries and greeted him with a smile on my face. "How are you doing, Bob?" Suddenly, without warning, I was lambasted with a string of descriptive swear words explaining the essence of his day. I stepped back as though I had suddenly been hit by a water balloon. Then I did something entirely out of character for me. I said nothing, turned around, and walked back to the relative warmth of my work area.

As a rather sheltered individual, I really am not accustomed to such profanity. I had grown up in a Christian home, went to Christian schools, and attended church and other Christian social events. Before this job, I had worked almost exclusively in Christian offices. When previously confronted by someone swearing, I had jacked the person up or corrected him, telling him not to use the Lord's name in vain. Both individuals defended themselves with a denial of one sort or another. But this time, I was overwhelmed and I kept silent. In the minutes and hours that followed, I asked myself, "How would Jesus handle this?" I don't think Jesus was so much into correcting sinners as He was into healing them. How could I step into the Healer's shoes and make a difference? His yoke is easy, His shoes are light.

I know a lot of you face this atmosphere daily. Sad to say, it is too often a part of the many military workplaces.

Cursing and the use of foul language are pretty sick behavior. I'm sure all of us would agree that nothing good comes of it. What I am really wondering, however, is what can I do as a Christian to change the atmosphere? Corrie ten Boom's sister in *The Hiding Place* lifted up this prayer in the barracks of a concentration camp where her roommates were fighting and bickering and filling the air with obscenities: "Lord Jesus, send Your peace into this room." Just now, at 11:47, Thursday evening, I ask the Lord to help me bring a bit of His peace into my workplace. I know I have nothing of my own to share. I would be the first Adventist to argue a doctrine or correct a foul-mouthed coworker. But this, I firmly believe, is not sharing His peace or witnessing.

"Lord Jesus, help me loosen the shoestrings of the heavy shoes of those around me. Amen."

CURIOSITY CAN . . .

Even the sparrow finds a home, and the swallow builds her nest and raises her young at a place near your altar, O Lord of Heaven's Armies, my King and my God! —Psalm 84:3, NLT

I watched the bluebird house with great interest after we nailed it to the fence that late spring day. Had we waited too late to put it out? Would any bluebirds even notice its appearing? After all, there never had been one there before. We watched from inside the house, sitting at the kitchen table hiding behind the horizontal window blinds, spooning in Shredded Wheat. Nothing happened for a few days and we agreed that the birdhouse, perched on the fence, probably would be vacant till next spring.

But then one day, the bluebirds came and checked out the housing. They stood cautiously on the fence, turning their brilliant feathers in the sun. Finally, after several days of inspection, the couple in blue moved in. Critters with and without wings came by to see the new tenants. Those colorful airmen stood their ground, even dive-bombing curious squirrels in typical Red Baron fashion.

Thinking of his new friends in blue, my husband, Don, cautiously mowed past their front door. Would he scare them away? He hoped not. He smiled when he talked about them and seemed to consider them real-life neighbors. He loved their spirit, their beautiful blue, their sheer tenacity for survival, and especially their choice of homes—in our yard.

Then one day, I, like Eve, let curiosity guide my footsteps. I wanted to see what was going on inside. Were they still there? I hadn't seen any activity around the nest, and it seemed like it was time for the babies of those feathered friends to have feathers enough to fly away.

I opened the back door and walked quietly through the grass to get a closer look at my neighbors on the fence. I stood in front of their house listening for chirping sounds inside the tightly sealed redwood abode, but everything was absolutely quiet—almost too quiet, like the absence of life. Quietness seemed to envelop me because I didn't even hear any cars go by on the road. All nature seemed to be holding its breath. Time seemed to stand still. Then I reached out my hand to release the clasp that held the door shut to check things out. "Surely they are gone," I said to myself, as I lifted the birdhouse door.

Inside there appeared to be a very flat bed of feathers. No, on closer look I knew it was a whole bird, but it was so still and flat, with its feathers out wide, that I wondered if it was dead. I shut the door quickly, thinking that whatever was going on shouldn't involve anymore of my attention.

Was it a dead mother bird? "No," I argued with myself, "that was no dead bird, that was a mother bird playing dead to protect her young." However, I wasn't absolutely sure. I also wasn't sure whether touching the door would keep the father away or scare the nesting mother. I tried to put the incident out of my mind. "Self," I said silently, "perhaps if we just forget about this, everything will be fine."

A few days passed and Don began to wonder out loud why his precious bluebirds weren't around. I kept quiet, hoping they would miraculously reappear and put to rest my greatest fears. How could I tell him what I had done? He talked about it again and again, and I could tell he was mystified by their disappearance. I was beginning to realize the awful truth. They weren't coming back! I must have scared the mother bird so much that she had fled from her home, abandoning her little family the minute I was out of sight.

I reasoned that I didn't know how many other predators had tried to disturb her nest. Wow, was I a predator too? What an awful thought! I loved those birds, but gazing on a family that hadn't invited me in put me in the jailhouse—big time. I imagined myself in a striped suit, pleading my case: "Judge, please understand. I wasn't trying to hurt them; I just wanted to look!" But my imaginary conscience-pricking judge slammed down his gavel, "You were an intruder to Mr. and Mrs. Bluebird! You threatened them—you. YOU!"

After almost two weeks of hearing Don express his dismay over the absence of his bluebird friends, I finally mustered up enough courage to tell my husband the truth. I confessed! He looked at me unbelievingly. I looked in his eyes for the hurt or the anger that I expected to see. I'm sure it was there, but what I saw was a heart on notice.

He now knew why his little blue buddies were gone—his other buddy, me, had disturbed their world. I told him I hadn't come to scare them, but I knew that to them, I appeared as a big giant, with the big eyes and a funny smell. How could they welcome that?

If I had come as a little neighboring bluebird, poking my beak in to say Hello, I wonder if they would have welcomed me and stayed to chirp. If only I had put out a bird feeder next to the kitchen window and watched from a safe distance behind those horizontal blinds, maybe the couple of blues would've stopped by and learned to trust me.

Jesus knows the answer to this dilemma better than anyone, for that is just what He did for us—He became one of us so we could learn to trust Him.

I sat alone at the kitchen window behind the blinds, looking out at the empty birdhouse. I wondered if they would ever return. Quietly, I asked God to give me another chance. I thought of the melodic words in a song, "His eye is on the sparrow and I know He watches me." This was no trivial matter. I knew that. I had transgressed the law of nature: Thou shalt not enter anyone's house smaller than yours, especially when not invited. A rain drop whizzed past me, then another. It might be God crying, I chastised myself. The dew had seemed extra heavy since my little journey into the deep realms of curiosity, terror, and silent lips.

I was so sorry. Never again would I let my curiosity muzzle my common sense. I knew then that curiosity can—kill! I looked up from my place at the kitchen sink. Outside the traffic raced by. It wasn't quiet this morning, inside or outside my heart.

Would I ever care for others, birds and humans alike, as God does? Leaving well enough alone or stepping in only when the Spirit calls? I didn't hold out much hope for myself, not yet. I dried the last dish and neatly hung the dish towel over its bar. Time would tell. Maybe next spring they would return. Maybe soon He would too.

RIP TIDES

Every summer of my Southern California childhood, our family would go to the beach for a week or two. Being naturally lily white, I welcomed the chance to get a tan, even to the point of enduring a few "peel good" burns. I made sand castles, attempted to body surf, and listened to the wild surf. I loved breathing in its wonderfully salted air. There were two things, however, that I really feared— tidal waves and rip tides.

I probably will never see a tidal wave except in the movies, but rip tides are another matter. The threat was very real. Those silent monster currents prey on unsuspecting deep waders and pull them out to sea, away from any possible help. The only rip tide story I remember personally happened on Lake Michigan when Keith Hannah, one of Don's best teachers, tried to save his dog. His little dog had jumped off the dock into the water and was trapped by an undercurrent and dragged under by a big lake rip tide. Keith loved that dog and without any thought for his own safety, he dived in and tried to rescue it. Horror of horrors, he was swept under with his dog and both drowned. It was hard to believe that a huge lake could harbor such a dangerous rip tide.

Sometimes, I think the words I utter are like those mysterious rip tides. Perhaps well-meaning information is passed on (the surface water looks fine), but I don't realize that someone may be hurt from my seemingly innocent sharing of negative information (the old rip tide). How often have I been surprised later on to learn the whole story, which has sometimes put the previous information in an entirely different light.

In Washington, D.C., there was a campaign against gossip, backed by a whole array of senators and congressmen (Reuters: "Group Launches Campaign to Reduce Gossip"). It was called "Words Can Heal." Some of the ideas behind the campaign are supported by the Bible, especially in Psalm 34:13: "Keep your tongue from evil, and your lips from speaking deceit" (NKJV). You might want to read the pledge below and pray with me that God will give us the strength to utter only words that heal—not words (whether true or false) that may pull another person down, like those insidious rip tides.

A Pledge to Think Before Speaking
(From the "Words That Heal" Campaign)
I PLEDGE to think more about the words I use. I will try to see how gossip hurts people, including myself, and work to eliminate it from my life.
I WILL TRY to replace words that hurt with words that encourage, engage, and enrich.
I WILL NOT become discouraged when I am unable to choose words perfectly because making the world a better place is hard work. I am pledging to make the world a better place one word at a time.

TINY BUBBLES

I sat in my manager's office on the tightly upholstered sofa across the room from his desk. Here I was in the "open door" office, as he had advertised it. A single tear rolled down my cheek. It had been a tough week and this little talk about my contribution to the suggestion box was not coming out as I had hoped. Instead, the manager's concern seemed not to be for his employees but for his own reputation.

Several things had happened already that day and now this felt like the last straw. Another tear silently rolled down my cheek and this time I tasted the salty liquid. I valiantly tried to keep my pleasant face mask on as he continued bemoaning being misunderstood.

I didn't feel very compassionate. Furthermore, I was proud of my comments.

They seemed so defined at the time, ending with "I am amazed and disappointed." Obviously, they had caught his eye too.

Finally, he had his say and I walked out of the office avoiding eye contact with the sweet secretary who sat silently at her desk. I walked down the long hallway and out the front door to my car. I slipped into the front seat, waiting the few minutes until my shift began. The sun beat down on my face, drying my silly tears.

I had been warned by Dear Husband that my comments to the employer would not be well received. But, as always, I felt driven to put my two cents in. Now, I realized that my words had "done me in." They were no big weather balloon of eloquent wisdom—just tiny, irritating bubbles. My thoughts kept me awake. *What can I do to make things better at work? How can I be a help to the manager instead of a squeaky wheel?*

Everyone is stressed these days—soldiers, sailors, airmen, and support teams as well. As I look at the many faces around base, I can see it. I laughed at myself for taking this little encounter so seriously and vowed to lift my side of the cloud. But I know, and you know, too, that we can't do this in our own strength. We might feel like it one day, but then the next, we might really feel depressed and just plain tired, physically as well as mentally and emotionally. Jesus has an answer for that. It also has been made into a song, and this song has power because it comes from Isaiah 40:31 in the Bible:

"They that wait upon the LORD shall renew their strength;
they shall mount up with wings as eagles; they shall run,
   and not be weary;
and they shall walk, and not faint."

Teach me how, Lord, to wait. This is my prayer; its melody circles my heart and lifts me up!

TIME OUT

I hurried back to the hotel's central computer and pushed the reject button for the master tape to change the day's record. Musing all the way around the room, I told myself I must be patient for just a few more minutes and then the job would be done. I knew it was a small thing, but so important.

But as I slipped my hand between the machine and the computer desk, my fat little fingers hit two buttons instead of one and suddenly the master computer turned off.

Oh, no! I thought to myself, and then quickly pushed the button to turn the machine back on. It looked pretty harmless, until I saw that I needed to input more information than I knew to get the machine up and running again. I walked to the front office to call the technician, wondering if I had done something really wrong, or if this little accident could be righted quickly.

As time went on, my question was answered. For the next twelve hours, the computers, laptops, and printers were silent—no output at all because my grubby little fingers had wavered from their destination, causing trouble for so many people.

There are times in our lives when we all make silly mistakes. We don't mean anything by it at the time, and we may not really stop to focus on what is important right then, whether it has to do with a machine or with a friend or even a stranger we have passed along our way. Each moment is like money in the bank, waiting to be drawn out and used to God's glory and our impending growth.

If we mess up, if we touch the wrong button or play a game with fate in some way, we do pay for it. You probably have felt the disappointment and the depression when things just aren't going as planned. The devil jumps up and down when he sees us hang our heads in shame or disappointment.

Jesus is not a traditionalist in this one, though. He's not big on punishment. He much prefers reconciliation and healing, if we want it. And you can be assured He is waiting. We just have to ask.

David was a man after God's own heart. He said it best, and his words weave their message in my disappointed soul like a river of joy:

"He makes me lie down in green pastures, he leads me beside quiet waters, he restores my soul. He guides me in paths of righteousness for his name's sake" (Psalm 23:2, 3, NIV).

Notes on . . .
Dealing With Human Emotions

Anger	*Fear*	*Joy*
Anxiety	*Grief*	*Sadness*
Disappointment		

BACK-STEP MEMORIES

And we know that all things work together for good to them that love God, to them who are the called according to his purpose. —Romans 8:28

One night long ago when I was a little girl, I slipped out the back door of our home on Tamarack Avenue in Inglewood, California. In the darkness, I slowly sat down on the back steps and looked all around me. I still remember the coldness of the cement step and what I saw high above me in the night sky.

As I looked into the heavens, a bright star attracted my attention. I began humming a simple tune: "Twinkle, twinkle, little star, how I wonder what you are. Up above the world so high, like a diamond in the sky . . ." My humming turned to vocalizing and I sang those words over and over, emphasizing different words each time around. It was like I was putting layer upon layer of blessings each time I sang another round. Everything was dark around me that night, but I didn't have any fear in my heart. After all, I was in my backyard and when I turned around, I could see the warm glow coming from inside my home. Right there on the cold steps under the clear sky, my thoughts focused on the future and what life would be like for me one day. I imagined great and wonderful things happening. It was as if I were on stage and the play had just begun. The anticipation was electric.

Years have gone by. The other night I again went outside and looked up at those same stars and realized that my dreams were pretty small compared to the blessings of life I have received. I am so happy to be alive, and I look forward to Jesus' soon return.

Lately, I've heard people talking about this and that fearful thing. You can almost feel the fear in the room. They see signs of the times unfolding. They share fear like an old hat, anticipating with a strange look the evil that will come upon the world. Of course, as Christians, we know a lot about earth's last-day prophecies as we rehearse these strange phobias in the midnight hour of earth's history. I think we forget the assurance that when we see these things come to pass, the Lord will come back to rescue us from this cruel world. It is wonderful! Jesus is almost here! He is coming! He is coming for me!

One reason I don't need to fear is that I am sitting on the back step of His home. He has the stars in His hands. In fact, He has the whole world in His hands.

The next time a fear monger tells you about all the evil man has planned for God's children, give them some Blessed Assurance. Tell them that, yes, these things are coming, BUT SO IS JESUS! Talk faith, not fear. We are about to break forth with song, and this time it won't be my dreamy "twinkle" song but the grand and majestic "Hallelujah" chorus. The apostle Paul reminds us "All things work together for good to them that love God" (Romans 8:28).

Never forget that—never.

IT'S TIME FOR BED

Through these he has given us his very great and precious promises, so that through them you may participate in the divine nature.
—*2 Peter 1:4, NIV*

The room was cool as I shifted my weight to sit up on the edge of the examining table. It was time for my annual physical and I was waiting for the nurse to give me a routine EKG. So far I had learned that I was shorter and fluffier than a year ago. Could it be that I was now in serious contention for the Pillsbury Dough—girl? Earlier I had been sitting in the office of my primary care physician, answering all kinds of questions about my health habits and family history. I blushed as I answered the question on regular exercise, realizing I really wasn't taking very good care of myself.

The previous year I had been nursing torn and frozen shoulder muscles, had gone through surgery, and graduated from physical therapy. Back in his office, my doctor asked me to raise my arms to see how I had improved. For a moment, I imagined myself as an Olympian on the winner's platform. The vision lingered momentarily but still I smiled inside, realizing how far I had come in the healing process from those first few days after the surgery. Sure, I was still some distance from feeling completely normal, but at least now I could use my arm, even to reach and attach heated curlers. Wow!

I thought of my mom and her loving care in my childhood. She was always there when I got hurt or felt lonely or just needed to talk. At the medical clinic, I was talking to a doctor, another female, who took great care to get the whole picture of my health. She reminded me of my mom, who continued always to find something humorous in a tense situation. She flashed me that winning smile of hers to let me know that there was no one more important to her. I'm sure my brothers feel the same way too.

Quietly, without complaint, mom has unselfishly shown us the heart of the gospel, that God loves us unconditionally and is with us, always. I wonder which is true—Does God have a mother's heart or do mothers have a special piece of God's heart? I'm sure Mom would advise me after that analogy, "It's time for bed!"

So I'll rest in Him and thank God for her. Happy Mother's Day, Mom!

A PLACE FOR MY HEART

"For where your treasure is, there your heart will be also."
                                        —Matthew 6:21, NIV

Snow swirled outside our windows as we filled more and more boxes with our belongings. I spied my childhood scrapbook covered in my favorite leopard skin design and decided to put it inside a nice attaché case to protect it.

On the table was a neatly written list of all the books in our pastoral library. I was proud of myself, for being so detailed and turned around to add the finishing touches on a box holding my favorite Thai fruit boat painting. "Ah, there," I said to myself as I added the cautionary words in bold print: "Fragile, price-less painting, handle with care!" Don and I joked about what we should sell of each other's prized items. I was willing to part with all the stereo equipment he had acquired at a military PX overseas, and he was more than willing to sell my china, special for its pattern, Inglewood, the same name as my hometown.

When the last box was loaded onto the van, we were ready to go! Don had just completed two and a half years of seminary training, and we were going west to spend Christmas with my folks before heading back east to our first church. The van was going to Georgia where the Savannah pastor had arranged for some men to unload the contents into a rental he had found for Don, his new assistant pastor.

A couple of weeks later, we found ourselves at our new Savannah apartment. I walked up to the door with our Schnauzer Fritzy in hand and suddenly time seemed to stand still as I noticed that the door was ajar. A sickening feeling came over me as I went in to find lots of boxes stacked up, some open and some empty. We went from room to room and noticed that many of our prized items were now gone, including Don's stereo, my china, the boat painting, my scrapbook, and almost our entire pastoral library.

Much later, we were able to laugh when we realized that someone, prob-ably unrelated to the thief, must have received a blessing from reading all those well-marked religious books. I have a feeling that when we get to heaven, Jesus, in order to help us understand our life here on earth, will introduce to us the blessed bookworm who ended up with our books.

Although we lost many things, priceless to us at the time, the blessings we received from the gifts from the local church and the seminary were priceless in themselves. I found that those things I secured in boxes weren't really my trea-sures after all.

Speaking of priceless treasures, I'm happy to say that Don, my husband of more than forty years, is certainly God's gift to me, followed by my beautiful daughter Steph and my loving parents. And last but not least, a gift I will cherish always is God's gift of eternal life, the greatest treasure of all time! And that, dear friend, is exactly where I want my heart to be!

GOD IS SO GOOD

> *I saw the Holy City, the new Jerusalem, coming down out of heaven from God, prepared as a bride beautifully dressed for her husband. And I heard a loud voice from the throne saying, "Now the dwelling of God is with men, and he will live with them. They will be his people, and God himself will be with them and be their God. He will wipe every tear from their eyes. There will be no more death or mourning or crying or pain, for the old order of things has passed away."*　　—*Revelation 21: 2–4, NIV*

The air was still fresh and it was quiet as we sat on the porch of our Texas ranch house. My little dog Missy, my friend for eleven years, sat beside me. She wasn't really breathing that hard right now, despite her failing heart. Though we were constantly moving in the army, Missy adapted well to all six of our homes from New Jersey to Korea and now in Texas. She helped make each house a home with her warm welcomes. That morning of July 1998, however, was different. That was the day we would take her to the veterinarian and have her put to sleep.

After she had undergone repeated seizures, I agreed she was experiencing too much pain, so I made the appointment. The day had arrived and the two of us sat there watching the sun come up. Out of the corner of my eye I detected movement in the empty field next door. I looked over waist-high tumbleweeds to see two deer standing perfectly still. They gazed intently at us for the longest time and then vanished into the fields. I patted Missy's head and stroked her silky white coat.

She relaxed and moved closer to me. Later that morning, Missy, sixteen-year-old Steph, and I piled into our old maroon Trooper for the long ride through the dusty hill country to the vet's office. Strangely, it seemed like any other day. Even waiting in the office for Dr. Bean seemed so routine. Then his assistant called us and I let Missy down to walk by herself on the shiny tile floor to the examining room for her final visit. She had no fear; she was with us—her caretakers, her family.

My heart started to pound as the finality of the moment set in. The vet and his staff were gentle in their words and actions as he explained what would happen. They held our little Missy and we patted her furry legs, feeling that warmth of her little paws. Then the injection started and she fell asleep. The life light literally vanished from her perky black eyes.

It was over. The room seemed sterile and cold now. We walked out into the Texas sunshine and the tears started to fall. Silently, I thanked God for Missy who was certainly His gift to our family for so many years. There is only one way down from the mountain of grief—gratitude to the One who makes life possible in the first place. God is so good.

Those of you who have had a pet and lost it, or still have a pet to interact with, know the close relationship that can develop. Some call these precious little creatures therapy dogs. I think that fitted Missy Snow Star, our Bichon Havanese. Some of her furry brothers and sisters have helped heal the very young and sick and the very old and senile. God knew what He was doing when He created them and had Adam name them, one by one.

Later we adopted a Bichon Bolognese puppy. Her playmate is a Cavalier King Charles Spaniel. They are only three days apart in age. We call them Missy and Ramona (but Steph calls the Cavalier Smokey Little G). They remind us just how much God loves us.

Occasionally, I've been asked if I thought our pets would go to heaven. Of course, I haven't found any scripture saying that, but I am confident that one day soon when Jesus returns, He will gather us in His arms and give us the desires of our hearts. We'll walk with Him and talk forever and a day of many things. Perhaps Jesus will restore Missy Snow Star, or perhaps something even better. I know for sure He will wipe away my tears and give me a long hug and fill my arms with something special to heal my silly heart. What a wonderful Savior!

GET DRESSED!

Finally, be strong in the Lord and in his mighty power. Put on the full armor of God so that you can take your stand against the devil's schemes.
—*Ephesians 6:10, 11, NIV*

An uneasy feeling swept over me as I emerged from another journey into my nighttime fears. My bedroom, the place of my torment, stands out clearly in my mind—downstairs, far away from my protecting parents, my double bed backed up against the wall, facing the open arched door to my toddler brother's bedroom, and the shadows beyond. On mornings like this, I felt so alone waking from a dream that would not go away. Its memory would sit in the lap of my childhood fears and weasel its silly face into my world.

Some of my dreams did make me feel small, but others made me feel larger than life. I laugh as I remember dreams of effortlessly jumping over telephone poles and then flying high in the sky looking down on nearby neighborhoods. The boundaries of my dreams were framed by homes next to the center of the place I knew the best—my own backyard.

Sometimes I would jerk awake, trying to rescue myself from a sensation of falling to my death onto the wooden floor beside my bed. At other times, I would waken uneasily from a dream that left me outside naked, somehow having forgotten to put on my clothes. I would vainly try to hide from no one and everyone in one big embarrassing gulp, until I escaped by waking up. In the foggy reasoning surrounding my dreams, I would always eventually face the big "V"—the state of feeling vulnerable, defenseless, and alone in the center of a full house of family.

Occasionally, I would gather my dreams like a box of clutter and ponder their meaning one by one, trying to learn something about myself. Now that I think of it, perhaps my eager quest to escape my nights explains why I love mornings so much. Mornings are beginnings. Sunshine erases the dark corners in my room. Getting out of bed takes me a step closer to leaving the scene of the crime and running to backyard pastures far from my fears.

One night at prayer meeting, as we were studying the book of Romans, a light seemed to go on in my mind as I read these words:

"But make sure that you don't get so absorbed and exhausted in taking care of all your day-by-day obligations that you lose track of the time and doze off, oblivious to God. The night is about over, dawn is about to break. Be up and awake to what God is doing! God is putting the finishing touches on the salvation work he began when we first believed. We can't afford to waste a minute, must not squander these precious daylight hours in frivolity and indulgence, in sleeping around and dissipation, in bickering and grabbing everything in sight. Get out of bed and get dressed! Don't loiter and linger, waiting until the very last minute. Dress yourselves in Christ, and be up and about!" (Romans 13:11–14, The Message).

"Dress yourselves in Christ . . ." The words just jumped out at me. They spoke words of hope like sunrise after nighttime shadows. I realized that as I come to Him, God gathers all my nighttime fears and tosses them like kindling into the fire of His presence. In my devotions, my time alone with Christ, I am actually taking time to dress myself in Christ, in the Word of His promises.

I can notify my silly heart that I no longer need to fear being vulnerable and have no need to fear the shadows, for I am covered with His coat of many promises. Why wouldn't I want to get dressed?

REMEMBERING HOPE

Be kindly affectionate to one another with brotherly love, in honor giving preference to one another; not lagging in diligence, fervent in spirit, serving the Lord; rejoicing in hope, patient in tribulation, continuing steadfastly in prayer. —Romans 12:10–12, NKJV

It was Christmas Eve, 1972, in Bangkok, Thailand. My husband was working late that night as an assistant to the chaplain of Crown Bowling Chapel, a U.S. military chapel for all faiths, in the heart of old Siam.

The day was hot and outside the little toys for tots had been passed out to the gathering orphans who had been smiling their way to "just one more gift from Santa." We felt good about giving to those grimy but smiling half-naked urchins, who never missed an opportunity to celebrate our holidays when there was something good to receive. But we, the Americans, the support troops for those in Vietnam? We were oh so homesick for an American Christmas.

Where was the snow? A better question was, When would the next monsoon hit mango land? You could set your watch by those! Where was the familiar sound of "Jingle Bells," "White Christmas," and "O Tannenbaum"? Oh yes, there was lots of glitter to buy at the floating markets, but where was just one good mall to gather up presents for good ol' Mom and Dad?

My husband said he had a surprise for me and not to miss the last Christmas program of the day, so I walked the half block to the chapel in the dark, feeling very alone and empty of any Christmas spirit.

As I stepped inside the fragile dwelling, I noticed the place was already filling up. The army chaplain was greeting the visitors warmly. I could see that—but suddenly to one side of the chapel, I did a double-take. "Who was that?"

The excitement grew inside me. There was a whole row of stunning girls, but that's not what caught my eye. In the middle of the row of lovelies, sitting quietly, waiting for the midnight Mass, was Bob Hope. He looked rather small next to big hairdos and spiked heels and flashy crowns. Actually, he looked remarkably ordinary.

Bob Hope! I said louder in my head. WOW! Out of his busy schedule, Bob Hope had come to our chapel, in the middle of the night, to share OUR silly Christmas. Suddenly, everything Christmas descended on that small little army chapel in the middle of bustling downtown Bangkok.

And we? Well, we had *Hope!*

NEVER ALONE

"The Lord himself goes before you and will be with you; he will never leave you nor forsake you. Do not be afraid; do not be discouraged."
—Deuteronomy 31:8, NIV

It was early autumn in 1994. I was taking my little dog Missy for her nightly walk outside the Servicemen's Center in Seoul, South Korea, which was our home for a year.

The Servicemen's Center was nestled inside the Korean Union Compound and at this time of night, all was calm inside the walls—except for the noise of traffic outside the compound.

One guest, who apparently had a lot of time on his hands, once counted six hundred cars, trucks, and buses passing by the compound in just one hour's time. Outside was the polluted, noisy, fast-paced Asian city of Seoul. Inside was a peaceful church compound after hours, where Missy and I were venturing alone in the semi-darkness of an empty parking lot.

As we walked farther toward Missy's favorite patch of grass, I cautiously looked over my shoulder for any movement in the dark shadows. I wasn't taking any chances of being surprised by some vindictive anti-American or deranged, starving Kung Fu activist. Perhaps I was a little paranoid, perhaps not. After all, twelve-year-old Steph and I lived at the Center alone, except for the gate guard who didn't speak a word of English. We were thankful for any guests who came to stay at the Center, often unmindful that we looked to them as our silent body-guards. What little faith I had! Here I was in Seoul, sent to direct the International Servicemen's Center by church officials who expected me to be a tower of strength and courage to young Adventist soldiers with communist North Korea just an hour's drive away. But, indeed, we did live alone, because Don lived a little over an hour away near the DMZ, where he ministered to the Camp Houze soldiers. And, believe it or not, this was the first time I had ever lived alone.

Missy and I walked on cautiously into the dark night. It was then that I thought I saw what appeared to be curtains or robes to my left. HIS robes? Beside ME? *I'd better just check myself into a mental ward—now I am hallucinating!* I chastised myself, laughing in muffled tones. Then I caught myself retorting, *Self, what little faith! But heads up, me of little faith!*

Gradually, a secure feeling swept over me like a warm blanket. I felt safe and loved and no longer alone. I headed back to the Center with a new confidence. Missy made no sound but obediently followed my steps. The warmth of experiencing the presence of Jesus filled my silly soul.

His words filled my head, "*The Lord himself goes before you and will be with you; he will never leave you nor forsake you. Do not be afraid; do not be discouraged.*"

THE HUG

Just a speck of me is Irish, given to me by my great-great-grandmother, a redhead born in Ireland. I love Irish potatoes and emerald shamrocks and could roll down any hill covered with clover and feel completely liberated.

My late brother Steve was born in March and often proclaimed his Irish connection. When Steve was born, I was confident that I would finally be the boss of something. My two older brothers had their share of trying to mold me to their will, unsuccessfully for the most part, but when Steve was born I saw promise in my leadership. It didn't work out that neatly, however. Steve was even more independent. When he was a little tyke, he would run like the wind to escape Mom and home. He didn't actually want to escape; he just loved to run. While in college, Steve completed the twenty-six-mile course of the famous Boston Marathon. I would've died in any long-distance run, but not Steve.

Growing up in Inglewood, I lived a stone's throw from Hollywood, so naturally, I dreamed of becoming a star. But brother Steve would howl and moan whenever I shared one of my new songs on my guitar. I'm not sure even today whether Steve actually was irritated by my voice or just teasing, but he did a good job of keeping me humble.

The last time I saw my little brother was when Don and I flew to Nebraska to sing for Steve and Sharilyn's wedding. When we entered the old college chapel, Steve greeted me with a big hug. We hadn't hugged much growing up, so it felt good. One week later, however, my little brother and his bride died in a head-on collision with a dump truck while returning from their honeymoon. We were devastated by the news and as time went on, I began working through the pain by writing songs such as "Simply Trusting" and "The Shout of Faith."

Out of the blue, ten years later almost to the day of their wedding, I was blessed with a vivid dream in which Steve stopped by and greeted me again with a big hug. It was so real that I woke up with a start and silently puzzled over what made me physically feel his hug. Then I remembered how a decade earlier on Steve and Sharilyn's wedding day, Steve encircled me with his big grown-up arms. The trauma following such a wonderful event apparently sealed that loving gesture in my memory.

Steve didn't realize it, but when he gave me that hug, he gave the best gift a sister could ever receive—love wrapped in a brother's strong arms. I am reminded in March each year that the gifts I give others last the longest when they are laced with love. One day my little brother is going to get his gift back. I promise![4]

TRUE COLORS

Consider it a sheer gift, friends, when tests and challenges come at you from all sides. You know that under pressure, your faith-life is forced into the open and shows its true colors. So don't try to get out of anything prematurely. Let it do its work so you become mature and well-developed, not deficient in any way. If you don't know what you're doing, pray to the Father. He loves to help. —James 1:2–5, The Message

I felt sick as I stared at the health report. How could this be? My body mass index, or BMI, was off the charts. I rebelled at the very thought and felt my waist again. How could I be so fat? Then I remembered what the health instructor said: "Some people don't realize just how fat they are. Skinny people can be fat inside too—and they are in just as much danger as visibly fat people."

I didn't feel fat. I did feel a little fluffy, but this score labeled me as "morbidly obese." I could die at any time. Would I have a stroke in my sleep? Fall away in a dead faint? I had no time to waste, except to worry like crazy because I had always considered myself relatively healthy.

Don joked with me about the score, whispering little phrases, "morbid . . . morbidity . . . *Ooobese!*" I looked in the mirror again. I never thought my little "rewards" would lead to this!

I saw Carolyn Lipscomb, one of the health testers, with the BMI monitor in her hand. "I just can't believe I am in the 'morbid' classification," I said. "Would you test me again?"

I stood still, as any Pillsbury Doughgirl should, while she had me hold the meter in both my hands. After a pause, she said, "Let me see your test results,

Nancy." She scanned the paper carefully and then said, with a tinge of humor in her voice, "Aha. Your height is listed as forty-five inches. No wonder you were put in that category. What's your height?" With a sense of impending joy, I answered, "Five foot five—sixty-five inches." Carolyn laughed. "You are twenty inches taller than this report shows. Your body mass index is not fifty-nine, but twenty-three."

I sighed in relief, feeling skinnier already. I straightened my shoulders and raised my head. Well, yes, I still needed to lose some weight but I was not— repeat, NOT—morbidly fat. Don mouthed the words again: "MORBID." Always a teaser, he was getting really good mileage out of this one.

I chuckled inside, not quite ready to release all the anxiety and depression that had built up. It would take a while before I could join Twiggy's skinny minis. I knew that. But I was free! I was no longer at death's door. Praise the Lord!

I thought of the many people who haven't had a miscalculation in their health tests. "Lord," I prayed, "thank You for letting me go through this trial. Help me to take time to improve my health and also to be more loving to others. Help me to look beyond a person's outside appearance to see the real person, their true colors, a treasure to God's heart!"

THE WAIT

It was summer and I perched like an owl on my suitcase with the emerald green grass of the Lynwood Academy campus spread like a carpet at my feet, as I waited for my parents to pick me up after a week at summer camp. I could still smell in the air the fresh cedars from camp and hear the sounds of other kids playing in the swimming pool.

For some reason, my folks had been delayed. I pondered the adventure of becoming an orphan but the beautiful afternoon scenes on this Christian campus lifted me past thoughts of abandonment.

It amazes me that even now I can isolate the moment and feel the warm sun and hear the delicate song of the leaves blowing in the wind. I was only nine years old and just a wee little blond kid with freckles.

The first night at camp, I remember feeling so homesick. Sure, it was fun being at camp, but I didn't know anyone. I later made friends with a girl named Sherry with jet black hair. She was larger than the rest of us and had a heart to match. But the most important thing to me was that she, too, was alone at camp. After that, I made it through camp with a new sense of freedom.

I had graduated from wilderness survival class learning to eat milkweed right off the growing plant. I smile when I recollect taking long walks with Jerry Dill, a singer from the Voice of Prophecy Quartet, on whom I had a crush. There were lots of other campers on those walks too, but I noticed only Jerry. He was a friendly star in my world and treated me kindly despite my schoolgirl crush, which would have been irritating to lesser souls.

But there I sat on this big academy campus that had been used for tent camp meetings, awaiting my destiny. I couldn't take a bus or hail a cab to find my way home. So I sat and I waited while within my soul grew a memory that I can still capture in my thoughts today. I'm sure you have cherished such moments in your life that live on. The outstanding ones are usually associated with some tragic event, such as the assassination of John F. Kennedy or the *Challenger* explosion.

Why did this little insignificant moment cling to my memory? I think it actually had to do with taking time to be alone with myself without artificial distractions. Even as modern, thoughtful, Christians, we don't take the time to be really alone. I don't mean a melancholy aloneness when the tears flow freely, but a time when we "Center Down" as the Quakers call it—a time when you throw all the worries and concerns of your life away or even better, give them to Jesus.

Some call it *Sabbath*.

SWEET IMMERSION

For all of you who were baptized into Christ have clothed yourself with Christ. —Galatians 3:27, NIV

I remember the ripple of the water, the mellow sounds coming from the organ, and the quizzical faces of my church family as I accepted Christ as my Savior in baptism. I was only nine years old, but becoming a part of the family of God will always be one of the most important times in my life.

I really felt a tremendous need to look for ways I could help others after that. This wasn't my natural self. You can just ask my brothers! Then, after Jesus came into my heart, I coveted any chance I could get to help other kids.

I can still see that Adventist elementary school courtyard so vividly in my mind, where we played jacks, tether ball, dare base, and other games. I remember distinctly coming to school that next week after my baptism feeling like a changed person. Oh, yes, I remember seeing the wary look of some church members who felt I was just another young student swept away by an ambitious young pastor. But I didn't see it that way, then or now.

It's been quite a few years since that big event at church and the humanitarian weeks that followed, but I still remember and cherish that feeling of wanting to be like Jesus. I can see Him kneeling beside His friends at the Last Supper and holding their feet tenderly, praying for each one. As Don said in one of his sermons, Jesus wasn't play-acting humility—that was just Him!

I wonder, when we get to heaven, will He wash my feet? Or will I get a chance to wash His feet? I hope I do! I want to hold His feet and like Mary, moisten His feet with my tears of joy and sweet release from sin.

SERMON IN SHOES

How beautiful are the feet of them that preach the gospel of peace, and

bring glad tidings of good things!   —*Romans 10:15b*

It had been a long time since I last went shopping for shoes, and when I found that perfect pair, I was delighted, inside and out—inside because they didn't cost much (the ten dollar price tag tickled my heart) and outside because they were so comfortable and cute. Cute doesn't often accompany comfort these days.

The first week I wore them, I stepped ankle-deep into a mud puddle just as we were about to visit someone and my perfect shoes were covered with Georgia clay. I was upset with myself for not noticing the puddle just below the car. How was I going to visit these friends with mud on the same shoes that would be walking on their fine carpet?

Fortunately, I noticed a garden hose just under the front steps and to my delight, I discovered that my perfect shoes were also rinsable!

Lately, I find myself taking special notice of other people's summer foot attire. Some wear precariously high heels to adorn their feet, in spite of the pain. Others wear shoes that must be pampered and avoid any contact with dirt, grass, or grease for fear that they would be disgraced permanently. Each pair of shoes reflects the tastes and needs of its owner. Each one touches the soul of soles of its occupant. Luxurious slippers or simple straps, they all tell some sort of story.

Many years ago, we sang about shoes at summer camp. There we were, lined up, a dozen guitarists strumming away to the catchy campfire tune "Do you know, oh Christian, you're a sermon in shoes? Do you know, oh Christian, you're a sermon in shoes? Jesus calls upon you to spread the gospel news. So walk it and talk it, a sermon in shoes." My dad loves the shoe song and has asked me several times to sing it again. I have even caught him singing the tune from time to time. I can see that it reminds him of the beautiful feet of those who bring *the* good news of Jesus Christ.

This is my prayer: "Lord Jesus, wash my feet with the peace of knowing that nothing can happen to me today that we cannot handle together."

THE SONG

The joy of the LORD is your strength.   —*Nehemiah 8:10*

A clear blue sky hung above us as we switched back and forth from riding elephants and walking the dusty trails into the hill country of Northern Thailand. Don and I had been invited by the Bangkok Adventist Hospital on their yearly hill tribe trip. We were to bring the guitar and share Christ in song with the hill tribes.

We had dined and slept the night before in the house of a local pastor. His warm hospitality had erased any apprehension we had of walking into the hills bordered by opium fields. The air was so cool and invigorating when we set out that it seemed as though we could walk forever without tiring. But as the tropical sun rose higher in the sky, we realized that the heat was sapping every ounce of energy we had. Oh, how we longed for any cool stream of water.

As I reached up to grasp a bit of brush going up one of the narrow shortcuts, the words from an old campfire song flooded my mind: "*The joy of the Lord is my strength, the joy of the LORD is my strength, the joy of the Lord is my strength, the joy of the Lord is my strength.*" [5] New surges of energy filled my failing muscles and it seemed as if the very utterance of the words were like streams of living water.

Just then we rounded a bend on the mountain and gazed upon the wide river below us. We ran down the bank, slipping and sliding while at the same time pulling out our bathing sarongs to slip off our clothes and bathe in the cool, clear shallows.

I still remember Don holding the colorful sarong between his teeth in an effort to bathe both his hands. Ripples of laughter cascaded from the bank above us from curious villagers. We laughed at these happy jungle people and settled down deeper into the pools, experiencing a little more privacy.

The words of the Scripture song kept wrapping their ribbons of joy around my head.

WAITING FOR THE TRAIN

"*Let not your heart be troubled; you believe in God, believe also in Me. In My Father's house are many mansions; if it were not so, I would have told you. I go to prepare a place for you. And if I go and prepare a place for you, I will come again and receive you unto Myself; that where I am, there you may be also.*" —John 14:1–3, NKJV

In my mind I can be there again, standing on the cement platform, suitcase in hand, not needing to look both ways—just waiting. Time stands still, sealed in my memory forever by the hopes and fears wrapped so tightly around me that dark San Francisco night in the early 1970s when Don was deployed to Vietnam.

One week, I was walking out of the exercise room at the Fort Gillem gym, when I glanced around the corner at the basketball court to witness a group of some twenty green-clad soldiers standing at attention in the center of the large auditorium. A handful of relatives, friends, and coworkers sat in the grandstand watching the formal ceremony of deployment unfold. I made my way across the bleachers as quietly as I could to sit behind some of these families.

In front of me was a young mother with her baby in a carseat beside her. To my left was a little girl with swinging hair sitting snugly against her mother as she waved her Barbie doll and a small American Flag in each hand. One lady behind me was dutifully videotaping the event. Another family sat arm in arm with an elderly gentleman who appeared to be one of the soldier's grandparents. Just one word brought the group of reservists being deployed to attention. They held their heads high, squared their shoulders, and clicked their heels together on command. The flag-bearer in front of the group straightened the official symbols of his unit on the guidons. The commanding officers took turns saluting each other as they gave over command, while I kept taking snapshots.

I saw something beyond the camera lens. I knew that outside this building, as with every other deployment, was a large bus waiting to take the soldiers to their destination. They were waiting for the train, in a sense. Memories of other wars came to the front of my mind—soldiers waving from open train windows to young wives or girlfriends standing alone on other cement platforms years ago. They had their traveling papers in hand and had accepted the call.

The title here says "Waiting for the Train," but instead of watching someone with a suitcase awaiting the arrival of the train, my eyes were on the ones waiting for the train to leave the station with someone very precious inside. It's a moment frozen in time. By the time you read this article, some things may be quite different. There is a big unknown out there and this silent dreading clings to us like sap from old trees.

You know what I'm thinking about right now? I want to think about waiting for Jesus. Instead of waiting for war, or for the economy to change, the gas prices to go down or, heaven forbid, another terrorist attack, I want to be standing on that train platform waiting for Jesus. After all, we do have this blessed hope! We wait or rest in faith in His promises and in His prophecies that tell us He is with us every step of the way. We are waiting, and this waiting makes the day you read this lifted way up high because we stand on the train tracks of this earth's history waiting for our Savior, our Redeemer, to return and lead us home!

MERGING MEMORIES

After months of living under the German comforter of overcast skies, the sun finally burst through the chapel windows that Sabbath morning. It was so beautiful that it warmed me inside and out. We were about to separate for the ordinance of humility—footwashing—before the Lord's Supper, when Don caught my hand and whispered in my ear, "Be sure and ask Stephi if you can wash feet together."

I silently sighed to myself, figuring that would be the day and remembering years ago also in Germany when a picture was taken at the Spangdahlen Air Force Chapel showing three-year-old Stephi eagerly washing my feet as her tiny dress dusted the floor.

I turned to find Stephi talking to her friends and put her on notice that Mom wanted to be her footwashing partner. She listened long enough to say she'd be down later. Silently, I walked to the door leading downstairs with my back to the group, feeling like I was in slow motion. Downstairs the ladies were already washing feet, and soon I found myself turning down invitations from dear friends, but keeping my eye on the door, with still no sign of her.

Finally, the group of ladies stood and joined hands in a big circle and right at that moment, in came Stephi. It seemed too late to be doing this; besides, everyone was watching, I thought to myself. But at the insistence of those dear sweet sisters in Christ and Stephi's sacrificial lamb-type willingness, we sat down with water, pan, and towel in hand.

The ladies continued to hold hands and they began singing. Scenes of Stephi long ago and Stephi grown up merged in one big lump in my throat. Soon she would be off to the military. Life would never be the same in our home, but we wouldn't trade the last twenty years for anything.

I did my best to keep my composure as we poured water on each other's feet, recalling a time some two thousand years ago when Jesus had done the same thing with His children, the disciples. He knew that life would never be the same in just a few hours for them either, and I'm sure He had a lump in His throat as He lovingly dried each of their feet, embracing them one by one.

My mind rejoined the present as I noticed the sisters surrounding us weeping as they sang. In that moment I could see they understood.

"Since we are surrounded by so great a cloud of witnesses, let us lay aside every weight, and the sin which so easily ensnares us, and let us run with endurance the race that is set before us" (Hebrews 12:1, NKJV).

Notes on . . .
The Future Home
of the Believer

Death: End or Beginning?	*The Colors of Heaven*
Mansions Bright and Blessed	*Come Unto Me . . .*
Redemption Draweth Nigh	

"TAPS" AND LETTERS

I pulled out my driver's license and ID card to hand to the guard at the gate. This was the third time this day I would be carded and searched. So goes the life of those of us entering U.S. military bases in Europe. But I wasn't in any hurry because I had my car radio tuned to an interesting program about patriotic songs. The soldier looked at my cards carefully and just when I expected him to motion me ahead, he looked me straight in the eye and stated that he didn't like that song. *What?!*

I was taken aback for a moment until I realized that "Taps" was being played on my radio. I took a closer look at this young man and could see he wasn't joking. He was just as young as my teenage daughter and suddenly appeared very vulnerable. In those few seconds we spent together, I shared with him that "Taps" was more like a bedtime lullaby to me, as I had heard it echo across the post every night at Fort Monmouth.

Then when I remembered the funerals, especially of a murdered chaplain's wife, the terrible finality of the song began to sink in. This song had been the theme of many funerals and no doubt the young guard could picture himself or his buddies in one. His openness brought me back to the reality of all this tightened security here and at home in the U.S.

Suddenly, I was swallowing hard. I became teary-eyed as I let up on the brake. What could I say? In those few seconds, we had met and shared his fears. I looked in my rearview mirror as I pulled away and there he stood in full battle dress: helmet, battle greens, boots, loaded rifle, and more.

Later that day, as I was picking up the mail at the Servicemen's Center, a black-rimmed letter with no address on it fell to the floor. Actually, it wasn't an accident. I was testing the ominous letter for any puffs of powder. Was this my "Taps"? No anthrax powder puffed from its corners, so I picked it up with tweezers, slowly opening the accompanying black-lined stationery. Again there was no powder. It was just a printed announcement of the death of my neighbor, Mrs. Hummel, at #16. I turned around to see another neighbor turning his back as if he had just witnessed the insanity of the moment.

In the distance, I could almost hear "Taps." I chuckled to myself and then thought, *I suspect that Jesus doesn't like that song, either. He has better songs for trumpets.* Then I began humming the tune to an old gospel favorite: "When the trumpet of the Lord shall sound and time shall be no more, and the morning breaks, eternal, bright and fair; when the saved of earth shall gather over on the other shore. When the roll is called up yonder, I'll be there."[6]

HOME MATTERS

And they shall build houses, and inhabit them; and they shall plant vineyards, and eat the fruit of them. They shall not build, and another inhabit; they shall not plant, and another eat: for as the days of a tree are the days of my people, and mine elect shall long enjoy the work of their hands. —Isaiah 65:21, 22

It was the close of camp meeting and we decided to take a little detour to visit our former home in Hixson, Tennessee. We drove past the church with memories stumbling over each other. At the top of the hill, we turned onto our street and headed toward the house we had lived in a little more than a year as a newly ordained pastoral couple, before going into the army chaplaincy.

"Stop, Don!" I motioned with my camera in my hand. "Let me get a picture of it!" I rolled down my window and started to take a snapshot of the cute little house at the edge of the sloping front yard. Just then the owner's wife saw us and motioned for us to come on over.

I took a picture or two and then we began a two-hour conversation about the old neighborhood and improvements made over the years. They were so excited to share their good fortune with us, even taking us out back to see their newly built red-roofed garage with vintage cars inside. Then they invited us inside their home to see how things had changed. The moment we walked in the door, something seemed strange. Was my mind deceiving me? I was sure things were a little different from when we lived there. Finally, we said our goodbyes and got into our car for the long trip home.

As we backed out of the driveway and turned toward the cul-de-sac side of the street, we realized that the home we had just visited was not our old home at all, but the one next door. The one that had been our home was dark and dingy and in need of much repair. We laughed at ourselves and headed down the street, too embarrassed to let that kind couple know we had just invaded their home and shared in their dreams without any real connection.

Every time we move, my mind goes back to the many homes we have lived in through the years. I've counted twenty-five-plus places, some nice, some not so nice. I remind myself that it is not the bricks or windows or doors that make a house a home. It is who lives there!

My dream of heaven used to include a fantastic house. But it isn't the house that matters—it's the home. And no place is really home without Jesus there!

HOMEWARD-BOUND CHILDREN

"Don't let your hearts be troubled. Trust in God, and trust also in me. There is more than enough room in my Father's home. If this were not so, would I have told you that I am going to prepare a place for you? When everything is ready, I will come and get you, so that you will always be with me where I am." —*John 14:1–3, NLT*

Every once in a while when I'm having trouble getting to sleep, I count houses instead of sheep. By the time I finish remembering details about each place, I'm fast asleep. But in these midnight musings, I forget to include the grand old houses of worship that have blessed my life each week. Many precious memories have been born there: baptisms, weddings, baby dedications, welcomes, and farewells of every kind.

Back in the 1950s, my little hometown was thriving. I'd see my friends at academy as well as at church. I remember so few things, but these have stuck in my heart: singing in the pew and choir loft; crying through Communion and weddings and dressing up in fancy clothes and stiff hairdos, to name a few. My church has certainly been a part of what I know as "home." I can still see the tall windows, the wooden benches, the lofty baptistry with its pastoral scene behind, the cement steps where we visited after the service, and the fellowship room where we drank hot chocolate after a chilly night of caroling.

It's true, my memories of home have taken me far away from my problems, but honestly, it is God's promises that I heard time and again at church that opened my eyes to His power and grace, giving me heavenly peace. It really feels like bedtime kisses that get me through the night. When Jesus promised "I will never leave you!" I feel safe. When He invites me to His home with "I have a place for you," I know heaven is not a fantasy, as the opening Bible verse above makes clear.

You can count on God when you can't fall asleep, for we are His homeward-bound children!

IT'S TIME!

Endings are so hard for me, God. They don't seem so painful for other people,
But everything within me cries out for sameness, community, familiarity.

New beginnings are scary for me to even consider.
Far away they are exciting. But up close, new beginnings terrify me.
Tonight, I am hating the responsibility of "yes" or "no" decisions that I am
facing.

Maybe my idealism simply can't handle clear-eyed reality—
The way I can't stand realistic movie endings that leave me sad, despondent,
    angry.

I want to be able to gaze clear-eyed. I want to be objective, level, with
    perspective.
Yet I hate the pain of ending a dream, a relationship, a good book,
    a lovely evening with someone.

There is a deep sigh that escapes from the depths of me
When I consider a new home, a new set of people, new values, new lifestyles,
    new goals.
I ache to stay with what is familiar. Mostly, I ache to stay with what is secure.

I struggle so with endings and beginnings, God. But paradoxically,
    I can't live without them.
Crises, changes, endings, beginnings . . . They are my source of life, direction,
    hope.

The above poem, "Endings" by Robin Williams, is one I collected while living at Fort Leavenworth, Kansas. I saved it all these years because it says a lot about moving pains. One day, after struggling to find just the right words to share relating to our impending departure to a new location and coming up empty, I finally I took my nightly walk with little Missy. The air in its freshness reminded me "all things will be made new." The street was empty of cars, bikes, and wandering dogs. *Everyone must be inside,* I thought, *quietly relaxing within.*

As Missy and I circled back toward home, I looked at all the houses and reminded myself how much I'd enjoyed walking in that neighborhood. Perhaps one day in the future on the "other side" (as we call California), I will go to sleep remembering these steps I took day after day in the South. I will remember how we ended each walk around the block. I'd call out to Missy as if training her for some great Olympic event: "Missy, it's time to go home!" I wanted her to connect the word *home* with our place, in case some dark night she found herself alone and didn't know what to do.

I laugh at my imagined victory as a dog trainer but pause in my amusement as I realize there is a double meaning to "It's time to go home." We all long at times to go where our hearts feel the warmth and security of childhood. But this "time to go home" reminds me that with Jesus, I can always make it safely through any storm, if I just remember that "it's time to go home."

When terrorism strikes again, I can rest assured that in times like these, "it's time to go home." When I sit by the sick bed of a dear friend, I can remember that Jesus also wants it to be a "time to go home"—whatever crisis, fear, or loneliness may plague me in the future.

Whenever I am homesick for Georgia, I'll know that God's angels, who also want it to be "time to go home," surround you and me. I'm going to memorize these words of Jesus: "Trust in God; trust also in me. In my Father's house are many rooms; if it were not so, I would have told you. I am going there to prepare a place for you. And . . . I will come back and take you to be with me that you also may be where I am" (John 14:1–3, NIV). You know, I really believe this: "It's time to go home." It's time to be together!

REMEMBERING THE MUSIC

God saves and will save me. As fiddles and mandolins strike up the tunes, we'll sing, oh we'll sing, sing, for the rest of our lives in the Sanctuary of God.   —Isaiah 38:20, The Message

It was the end of a great ministerial retreat in the mountains of North Georgia's Cohutta Springs Camp. The last song was still ringing in my ears as I filed out of the once-crowded room deep in thought. "Wow!" I said to myself. "This I will always cherish." It had been truly a sabbatical in the life of this pastor's family.

All the elements of rest were there: quiet times to drink in the silent songs of nature, mingling with new and old friends, handing out hope in a basket of conversations, and embracing time to really focus on God's love, care, and healing all mixed into one.

But the final song of the retreat still rang in my head. In fact, it had enlarged its surround sound of memories and spilled into my heart. Sometimes a song sticks in my mind for years, like fine lotion, soothing the edges of a day, softening the surface of seemingly fruitless times. This song was doing it again. *"Sing the wondrous love of Jesus . . ."* Inside I felt the warmth of His everlasting love.

"Sing His mercy . . ." Oh, how I knew He had given that to me. *"And His grace . . ."* I could almost taste His pure, transforming grace, sweeter than honeycomb. In my heart I touched His big, bold hands, scarred by the nails.

"In the mansions, bright and blessed . . ." Thinking of the next move was a bit overwhelming, but looking further ahead had its advantages. My heavenly Father, the God of the universe, was preparing a mansion, the best of all the houses we would ever live in, for me, silly old me! *"He'll prepare for us a place . . ."* A place, a single, personal space, just for me. It would be so personal and so detailed because no one else knows me better than Jesus!

"When we all . . ." I could still see those friends—new and old, men and women—standing like trees in a forest, strong and willing, lifting their hands and hearts toward the Son, *"get to heaven, what a day of rejoicing that will be."* Now, in my mind's eye, I could do it, stretching my arms out wide, my face washed by the sunlight of His smile. The whole world was revolving in the ever-encompassing splendor of heavenly music.

"When we all see Jesus . . ." Oh, this scene inside my heart was unbelievable.

Jesus standing before me, little old aging me! JESUS standing in flowing white robes and crowned with a mantle of white hair, looking into my eyes, with a smile so enthusiastic that it bordered on delightful laughter.

"We'll sing and shout the victory!"[7] YES, Yes, yes! It was ending too soon. But it was stronger than any million-man march shouting in unison. It was deeper than the sigh of a mother's relief. It was even wider than a Texas sky.

Even now, it circles the globe of my heart and lifts me up—to sit a while, again, with Him. Thank You, Jesus!

LIFT UP YOUR HEADS

> *Behold, He is coming with clouds, and every eye will see Him, even they who pierced Him. And all the tribes of the earth will mourn because of Him. Even so, Amen.* —*Revelation 1:7, NKJV*

It was quiet inside as I sat alone in the military chaplains' home where we were guests. Silently, I watched the rain coming down in sheets. I had never experienced this before and the moisture seemed to hang in the air like a scene from *Gone With the Wind*. Meanwhile, this Southern Californian had just been transplanted in the South by virtue of love and marriage and was feeling a little homesick for the California Sierras. Outside, all I saw was miles and miles of lush, green foliage on—flat land.

It was August 1970, and I had been in Georgia just a few days when I began thinking about my mountains. Finally, the rain had stopped and I ventured outside to hunt for something interesting. The warm, moist air engulfed me and I breathed deeply to relax.

Then I saw them just above the Georgia pines—gigantic participants on patrol, witnesses to nature's fury. The clouds continued to move across the pristine blue sky like marching soldiers, yet no two were alike. They appeared pompous, holding their territory with dignity and pride.

Far below, junglelike sounds began to emerge after the storm. Birds sang, crickets clicked their wings, and as the sun began to sink lower in the west, a whole parade of colors danced in the sky. I was hooked, for I had found a replacement for my mountains. Each day thereafter, I searched the sky for more Dixie surprises.

Since those early days in Georgia, I have spent many afternoons focusing in on the sky around the world. Sometimes I think back on ancient times when God spread His rainbow of promise in the clouds. I remember stories of when God used clouds to express His anger, to hide Moses from His presence at Sinai, and to cover His glory in Israel's wilderness sanctuary. I think of when God sheltered His people from heat and enemies, or blinded others to preserve His own. It is then that I remember that one day soon a little dark cloud will appear far off in the heavens. As it nears the earth, the small dark cloud will transform into a beautiful armada of heavenly angels surrounding our Savior.

I believe Luke 21:28 says it best: "And when these things begin to come to pass, then look up, and lift up your heads; for your redemption draweth nigh."

GOING HOME

One evening when everything was quiet at my place of work on the night-shift, I pulled out a favorite story magazine and read these words about an airman who was being detained by the Chinese government: "Alone, I passed the hours with my memories, in my mind going home even if I couldn't in actuality . . ." Lieutenant Shane Osborn.[8]

When I was little, I couldn't imagine ever leaving home. It seemed so terrible that I might someday be apart from Mom and Dad. Sometimes I would follow them around the house wondering how they could have grown up and left home. Then I met Don and fell in love and he became my home. I was so happy to follow him anywhere, to scores of homes around the globe.

Sometimes, however, when I think about Mom and Dad, I have wanted to be able to take a quick trip home and sit down at their table like old times. No one makes food taste better than Mom! When I think about them and have trouble falling asleep and escaping my racing thoughts, I will mentally take "The Trip." I will turn the corners, stop at the stoplights, look to my right at the taco store, and drive down the California freeway to just the right exit. Eventually, I will come to Felice—their street—turn the corner, stop the car, walk up to their front door, and peek into their kitchen window. By the time I have finished rehearsing the trip home in my mind, I have drifted off to the land of sweet dreams and heavenly reunions.

There are times in the swirling wickedness and greed of this world that I am lonesome for heaven, too. I long to be with my heavenly family—the Holy Father, the Redeeming Son, and our Comforting Holy Spirit—and get that long awaited family hug. That's when I begin rehearsing the road home. I can see myself standing outside the Servicemen's Center in Frankfurt, looking up at the sky, and seeing a small and seemingly dark storm cloud come closer and closer to Johann Klotz Strasse, my former street. My body shivers with anticipation and wonder as the cloud seems to come right over my head, but then I am relieved and filled with awe as the dark cloud of the future unfolds into a brilliant light that fills every corner of my vision. My eyes adjust to the light as I call His name, the holy name of Jesus. He answers me, clearing away the wispy clouds that separate us, and letting me see Him face to face. The angels around Him begin singing a beautiful song in an unbelievable harmony. His voice rises above the rest as I hear Him singing my name, MY NAME! —calling me to Him. "Nan, come to My house, come to the Marriage Supper of the Lamb." I suddenly feel weightless for the first time in my life, minus the leg cramps and shoulder pains, and those wonderful middle age pounds. The winds of a thousand years lift me up to Him and I take hold of His nail-scarred hands and look directly into His kind eyes as

He hugs me—He actually HUGS ME!—and I feel complete, whole, young, alive, just really good! We ride the winds of time to the New Jerusalem with family, friends, and strangers alike, laughing and singing and sharing the goodness of God. We travel through the corridors of time to our heavenly home. Jesus knew we would feel smothered with the heaviness of this world when He said these words in John 14:1–3, in the New King James Bible (I've added a few exclamations to help you take in each phase):

"Let not your heart be troubled *[It's all right now.]* you believe in God *[Right?]*, believe also in Me.

In My Father's house are many mansions *[There's a room for you!]*;

if it were not so, I would have told you *[I'm not kidding.]*

I go to prepare a place for you *[Your name is on the door.]*

And if I go and prepare a place for you, I will come again *[Because I AM coming back.]*

and receive you to Myself; that where I am, there you may be also *[By my side, FOREVER]*."

PILLOW TRIPS

"I tell you, I will not drink of this fruit of the vine from now on until that day when I drink it anew with you in my Father's kingdom."
—Matthew 26:29, NIV

In the middle of the night when I can't sleep, I take a journey in my mind. I relive a trip I took when we stayed at the Camp Pendleton guest house in California a few years ago. I imagine myself getting out of bed while everyone else is sleeping. Next, I'm lathering up in the shower and dressing.

I open the door, enter our rental car, and head out of the parking lot, first turning this way and that way down the road for the next thirty minutes. I can see the burrito stand, the bridge, and the other turns in the road. I can even smell the fresh fruit trees as I pass by in my mind.

Finally, after several miles of winding through the back roads of Escondido, California, I drive onto I-15 and head south toward my parents' home. It's just about then, without fail, that I cease my imagining and fall sound asleep. The next thing I realize is that morning has come, as the new day's sun is peeking through our bedroom window blinds.

From time to time, I've tried to map out other memorable routes, but it just doesn't work like my trip home. Those other scenes are just snapshots by comparison.

When I was a little girl, I became very lonely thinking about growing up. The thought of leaving home was absurd. Why would I want to do that? But as I grew older and gained some independence, I began to venture out farther and farther. I didn't feel homesick anymore, especially when I met True Love Don. But sometimes, when the nights are long and millions of tasks roam through my head battling for my attention, I just have to take another trip home. Everything quiets down as I make the journey.

I wonder if Jesus feels homesick for us. I wonder how often His heart turns to thinking about all His friends down here on earth. One day soon, Jesus will take a trip with millions of angels. As He gets closer to earth, He will see the beautiful blue sphere that has caused heaven so much pain. But His heart will rush to gather us up in His arms and take us home.

I remember Jesus' words at the Last Supper in the upper room when He promised His friends, the disciples, that He would wait till they were all together again in heaven to drink of the fruit of the vine. He was speaking of the traditional Passover and the emerging Communion service at the time.

He promised that His next Passover/Communion service would be when all His children were together again in heaven. I can imagine that until then, Jesus loves to think about us. He remembers our faces. He tastes our tears and is moved by our joy and laughter. He doesn't have to imagine things or try to drift off to sleep, but He always has us in His heart.

THE HUMMER

I saw Heaven and earth new-created. Gone the first Heaven, gone the first earth, gone the sea. I saw Holy Jerusalem, new-created, descending resplendent out of Heaven, as ready for God as a bride for her husband. I heard a voice thunder from the Throne: "Look! Look! God has moved into the neighborhood, making his home with men and women! They're his people, he's their God. He'll wipe every tear from their eyes. Death is gone for good—tears gone, crying gone, pain gone."
—Revelation 21:1, 5, The Message

I sat in the backseat grinning from ear to ear as Dad lowered the coral hardtop into its trunk. There we were, our whole family, slowly traveling down the Harbor Freeway in our new car, a Ford Skyliner convertible. I remember that car so well! We called it our "parade car" for the few times we drove down the street, radio up high, waving at people standing on the sidewalk in our little hometown. What a memory!

During college years, my brother Dennis and I shared a '56 Chevy (gas was thirty cents a gallon). Later, after Don and I were married, we started with the unforgettable green Rambler Hornet, and then others followed: a VW camper with a heater for Michigan winters; a Ford diesel Taurus that we sold when we headed for Germany; and a used BMW that taught us how to feel the road.

Many other vehicles came later. In Germany, Don had the privilege (due to lack of personnel) to drive his own military vehicle. In fact, he won an award for the soldier with the most miles traveled in a military vehicle without an accident.

Every day, Don would take off in his military vehicle, headed to one of his remote Army Air Defense Artillery sites where he ministered as the chaplain. The car he drove then was an ugly green, broad-bodied, all-terrain vehicle called the Hummer. Unlike today's Hummers, it didn't have the fancy seats or smooth-as-velvet ride. It was our rough rider, you might say.

But years have gone by and the Hummer has changed. Recently, we took a test drive in a new Hummer. It wasn't jungle green but bright yellow. Sitting in the backseat in quiet comfort felt more like riding in a Cadillac than the military vehicle of earlier years. It was still called the "Hummer," although you might call it the resurrected model. Thanks to some very generous people, we now own a small collection of miniature Hummers, which we cherish!

Sometimes when I look in the mirror or watch an elderly citizen walking haltingly in the mall, I think how different heaven will be. All the emotional burdens, physical aches and pains, sleepless nights, and agonizing days will be gone. We will still be us, but we will be restored to the image God intended for us when He first created our great-grand ancestors, Adam and Eve. We will look like our Father—the King of the universe. We will laugh with Him and grasp life with the energy of a newborn baby. We will be blessed with eternal life and walk the streets of heaven without a care in the universe.

Right now, wherever you are, take a moment to visualize your heavenly home. Imagine yourself face to face with Jesus. Breathe deeply and capture the sweet aroma of heaven. "Hum the Doxology," as Don would say. In a world that grows darker each day, perhaps this is the time to become a real hummer. Just start humming; hum to Him a melody of praise, holding on to every note as you ride the waves of grateful memory—and know that God is sitting right beside you because He promised He will dwell in the praises of His people.

THE COLORS OF HEAVEN

Look, he is coming with the clouds, and every eye will see him.
—Revelation 1:7, NIV

I love bright colors, especially in clothing, and have always thought of black apparel as most appropriate for funerals. As an American woman, it is important to have at least one black dress or suit to be ready for an unexpected funeral or solemn occasion.

However, when I was in Germany, I became aware that Europeans, as a whole, seem to wear a lot of dark colors. At first, I saw this as quite boring, but as time went by, I began to view it as smart and fashionable. After all, the women I saw in downtown Frankfurt were professionals, and they could be seen everywhere in the city. It began to dawn on me that black was also a great color to camouflage my nationality so I wouldn't stand out. There is a term for that in the military community abbreviated OPSEC: blending with your environment with your attire, attitude, and language—not giving away important military information in casual conversation, fading into your surroundings.

When I wore black, I wore all black. That included no white tennies or anything. Tennies would give me away every time. If I dressed in black and kept quiet, I could pass as a German national. This same principle wouldn't have worked for me in Korea, you understand; there aren't many blond Orientals, but in Germany, I was able to fit right in—if I wore black.

Needless to say, I adopted the color and my black wardrobe expanded during my years in Europe. When I became homesick for bright colors, I would satisfy my love for color by rationalizing that black is actually a combination of all colors. I visualized blues, yellows, reds, and greens all being dumped in one big vat and stirred into mystic black. That mental picture helped give my artistic side a bit of comfort.

I'm sure you've seen pictures of black holes in the universe. I think of Orion, one of the most beautiful constellations and legendary as the entrance to heaven. There is such brilliant light at its center that it appears black at that spot. I like to think of Jesus returning to earth from that dark spot in Orion.

When Jesus comes, He won't be wearing black, I'm sure. All of heaven will be arrayed in robes of pure white and Jesus and His angels will come with fire and trumpets and rainbows. I would venture that there will be a lot of lightning and unbelievably beautiful music surrounding the earth. When that day comes, I'll trade my black suit for a robe of white that will reflect unbelievably beautiful colors of God's own creation.

Oh, yes, Lord—come.

THE MOVER AND SHAKER

"Do not let your hearts be troubled. Trust in God; trust also in me. In my Father's house are many rooms; if it were not so, I would have told you. I am going there to prepare a place for you."   —*John 14:1, 2, NIV*

This scripture came to me in the dark of night. In my bedroom, circling me like a wagon train, were all of my boxes beckoning to be moved. The demons of unpacked belongings from other rooms seemed to call for immediate action.

How many times had I done this before? I started counting by cities: Columbus, Bangkok, Berrien Springs, Savannah, Atlanta, Macon, Thomasville, Hixson, Lawton, Fort Sill, Herforst Germany, Fort Monmouth, Columbus again, Fort Leavenworth, Fort Monmouth again, Seoul, Stockbridge, Ding Dong, Frankfurt, Stockbridge again, and now Winder, Georgia.

"Wow, you should be an expert by now!" I muttered, looking at the remnants on the floor, the pictures on the wall—oh, no, the closets. Lurking there were unmentionable amounts of belongings—precious, semiprecious, and downright junk!

If only I could have my army movers and packers again! They would pack it all. I remember one time opening a box and finding a wastebasket full of garbage all neatly packed away—and fossilized. "Lord, take it ALL away," I silently petitioned. "Clean my house! Not just the one on Arbor Cove Court, but the one inside." Jesus' words surrounded my heart, *"I go . . . to prepare . . . a place . . . for you."* Wonder of wonders, He promises to prepare it all.

As I mentally reviewed the various stages of moving, I suddenly realized that I didn't need to pack a thing! Not that Jesus would pack it; oh, no, that wasn't it. I could leave it all there—there at the Cross. *"Come unto Me, all of you who are heavily burdened."* I chuckled as I thought about my new home in heaven. Jesus would prepare my spice cabinet; can you imagine the aromas! He would give me fresh, fluffy towels and so many unbelievable things. My bed wouldn't need much attention because, after all, I wouldn't have to sleep at all—no droopy eyes, no yawns, no tired legs. I laughed again. And my windows would be crystal clear—no, not just crystal clear, they would BE crystal!

Someone out there in cyberspace may think this little diatribe (new word) is silly, but to this womanly soul, the one in the midst of unfinished packing and a myriad of unthought-of things to do, the thought of Jesus "preparing" a place, a home for me, is utterly fantastic. It is good news!

There is one overnight bag I want to pack, however. I want to put my family, Don and Steph and my little dog Missy, Mom and Dad, my brothers and brothers-in-law and their families, my church and chapel families from past and present, in there—and just one picture from my heart of Jesus kneeling in Gethsemane—the great Mover and Shaker of all time!

GOOD NIGHT, GRACIE!

I sat intently by the TV watching George Burns and Gracie Allen entertain us with their comic interpretations of everyday life. But the lines they spoke at the end of every program were the ones that we remember the most: "Good night, George." "Good night, Gracie."

When I was growing up, I had the luxury of staying in one city, with one church and church school family, for nearly twenty years. I knew everyone and they knew me. I could walk down the streets of our busy little town of Inglewood, California, and feel at home. But while I was in college, my folks moved to Escondido, about a two-hour drive from my hometown.

We settled into that bedroom community north of San Diego nicely. Then I went to college far away in Michigan, while still cherishing the memory of the beautiful desert breeze that tumbled over the open fields into the windows of our new home.

Then I married and embarked on the adventure of a lifetime. We moved every two or three years and had a great time. In the military, then the pastorate, then the military again, we traveled and lived in lands around the world I never imagined I would ever get to see. I never felt alone in these places, however, because Don and I were together. When Stephanie was born, we really felt like one big family. The three of us could make any place a home in short order. We became rich with friends and a multitude of memories gathered in our hearts.

When we retired from the military, I thought our adventuring was over, but instead, we were given the opportunity to travel again and to meet new friends all over, by being directors of the Seventh-day Adventist Servicemen's Center in Europe. We put all our belongings in storage in Texas, taking just three suitcases. When we arrived in Frankfurt, Germany, the center director, Chaplain Chet Jordan, greeted us at the airport, and we took off down the autobahn in Danny Edween's Volkswagen van to our new home.

Our "tribe" increased as we met and grew to love all who attended Adventist chapels around Europe in the military community. We lived through 9/11 and experienced a beautiful coming together. We watched in awe as hundreds of incoming soldiers, airmen, and seamen landed in Europe to fly off again.

When our daughter Stephanie entered the Air Force and flew back to Texas for basic training, it was hard to see her go, to turn the page in our family book, to know that she was beginning a new life on her own, without us.

As our two years of Adventist volunteer service ended, we decided to return to the U. S. It was a simple decision just to pack up a few things and go, right? We realized that although we might pack up a lot of boxes, we were leaving behind a part of ourselves like never before. We would be parting from people that we had come to know as our family and dear friends. We were so proud of the many helpful members and friends who lightened our burden and warmed our hearts. Each one was precious in our hearts and in His sight.

The old house, lived in by directors' families since the 1960s, brought to each of us chosen to govern it a special gift. Unlike the other homes we vacated, it would not be hollow and empty when we shut the door for the last time. It would be just as vibrant and alive as ever with people, loving people. It's because the Spirit of the Lord was there, surrounding each of us with the love of Jesus. He continues to keep the "light on" for all of us.

Like George and Gracie, I want to think that when I said Goodbye to the house, it was more like a mom or dad saying good night as they tucked their children into bed for the night. After all, it's just for a little while and when the morning comes, we'll see each other again. So it is with a little smile and a catch in my throat that I end this installment with these words: "Good night, Gracie!"

HOME IS WHERE . . .

I saw Heaven and earth new-created. Gone the first Heaven, gone the first earth, gone the sea. I saw Holy Jerusalem, new-created, descending resplendent out of Heaven, as ready for God as a bride for her husband. I heard a voice thunder from the Throne: "Look! Look! God has moved into

the neighborhood, making his home with men and women! They're his
people, he's their God. He'll wipe every tear from their eyes."
—*Revelation 21:1–4a, The Message*

Floating on my back, I watched the clouds roll by. They moved swiftly as if in a race, ever changing, ever forming and disappearing without the slightest sound. Since coming to Texas, I had found that the Big Sky gave new life to these ordinary objects of nature.

For the first time in our military housing experience, we lived far out from the city. We could see millions of stars at night without the street lights to dim our view. The only sounds we heard were from the animals: birds, cows, chickens, crickets, and owls—all having their say.

Sometimes I'd sit on the porch at night and close my eyes, listening to the wind blow through the huge scrub oak out front. The swaying of its branches sounded like the return of endless ocean waves. By the time I settled snugly underneath my bed covers, I could almost taste the salt air. We had definitely been blessed to live in that home in Ding Dong, Texas.

If I think back, I can picture every home we've ever lived in as a married couple. From our very first one, a small duplex with the out-of-tune grand piano, right outside the gates of Fort Benning, to this very big one, a three-story servicemen's center with a full basement in Frankfurt, Germany. All the homes hold a special memory of one type or another.

All of them symbolize another part of life's journey. Usually, we entered them empty and left them empty, at least free from our personal possessions. Their walls seemed cold when we arrived, warm while we were there, and cold again as we departed.

At the end of a stay from a few months to a few years, I would say Goodbye in a quiet sort of way and shut the door and look forward with anticipation to another adventure. It was good, it was melancholy, it was part of the rhythm of our lives. You know the feeling.

One day soon, when Jesus comes, I want to move into a home, put up my new favorite things, and stay a long, long while. I don't see that happening before my heavenly home, but that's OK. Home is where our heavenly Father sends us.

Notes on . . .
Experiencing God's Presence Everywhere

In a Cathedral	In Disasters
In an Airliner	In an Underground Cavern
At Taco Bell	In a College Dorm

In a Cathedral
Aboard an Airliner
At Taco Bell

In Disasters
In an Underground Cavern
In a College Dorm

A CARPET OF ROSES

Oh let the Son of God enfold you, with His Spirit and His love, let Him fill your heart and satisfy your soul. Oh let Him have the things that hold you and His Spirit like a dove will descend upon your life and make you whole. Jesus, oh, Jesus, come and fill your lambs. —"The Spirit Song"[9]

I looked out the airplane window that gray day in 1985, following the wall that divided East and West Berlin, with wondering eyes. It was easy to follow its path because of the wide swath of territory called "No Man's Land" that separated the two Berlins. I felt so small up there in the plane, but so blessed. Below me was a wall that represented sadness and separation for so many families.

Its message rang clearly for me: We are so blessed to be Americans, yes, and Americans living overseas. There in Germany, I was an American. In the states, I don't think about that. To those around me, I am a Californian, a Michigander, a Texan, a Georgian, etc. Living outside the United States helped me realize how unique our freedoms are. There are many beautiful lands that I enjoy visiting, but nowhere is there a freer land—this side of heaven, that is.

In the spring of 2001, I again ventured into East Germany. That time there were no walls to limit my travel. Instead, brand-new, expensive highways stretched for miles in every direction. New strip malls lined the autobahn with plenty of McDonald's popping up routinely. We went only a ninety-minute drive south of Berlin to Lutherstadt, Wittenberg, the cradle of Protestant Christianity.

Patches of the old neglected buildings were scattered throughout the city. They were stark realities of another time, begging to be forgotten. But even with these contrasting facades standing side by side, another, older era was standing taller and shouting louder. Into every age God shines His light of truth and grace. None is inferior, but only an older or younger brother to the other. Throughout the ages, God continues to unfold a revelation of His love. It's like God just keeps picking petals off the flowers, "I love them, I love them yet, I love them . . ."

Our last stop on the tour was at the famous Wittenberg University where

Luther and his colleagues courageously shared the gospel. Above the door was a sculpture of a healthy baby leaning on a skull. It looked a little strange to me until our guide Carina translated the words below it that in essence said, "Life is short." Inside, Carina drew our attention to the Luther Rose and the calligraphy encircling it on the ceiling. As she read the words, the room seemed to fill with a sweet aroma: A Christian's heart walks on roses when it stands beneath the Cross.

SWEET SILENCE

The last time we lived in Germany, we were able to take a trip to Israel with one of our chapel groups. We drove to the airport from Spangdahlem AFB, parked our car, and checked in at Frankfurt International Airport, at the El Al Airline counter. It was there that we entered the world of super security. We experienced for the first time the art of strip searches, endless questioning, luggage shakedowns—all things that seem almost routine these days.

As we walked onto the tarmac toward our plane that November day, we viewed an awesome scene. Commando-type guards were stationed in a large circle around the airliner with guns to their chests. I walked slowly, trying to take in the whole scene. It really took my breath away!

Once we boarded, there was no further evidence of high security until we entered Israeli air space, and there, two fighter jets escorted us to the Tel Aviv Airport.

Leaving the airport after the tight security and entering the ancient Holy Land with all its history was a trip in itself. I was entering the land of my childhood storyhour, and I felt as if I had stepped back in time. But the scene indelibly etched in my heart is the day we visited the Garden Tomb site.

The town had seemed so noisy and the crowds anything but reverent, but when we walked through the gate to this replica of the tomb where Jesus was buried, I felt a sweet peace surround me. His Spirit was there and, I was certain, a whole legion of angels was surrounding those who visited.

I felt safer at the Garden Tomb site than at any other time during the whole trip, coming or going. We sat down on some cement benches, in full view of the empty tomb, on the other side with our friends, Adventist Chaplain Larry Smedley and Presbyterian Chaplain Fred Carr and his wife, Sharon. There we took the precious Lord's Supper together in the shadow of a tomb that was like His.

We were quiet, too, remembering the view when we peeked inside the empty tomb. It was so quiet. There were no golden arches or ornate crucifixes there—only silence, sweet silence. In my mind, too, I could hear the words to a song:

> *"Come with me to the tomb where He lay. See the stone, it's been rolled away. Death could not keep our Savior in. He rose from the tomb to save us from our sin."* [10]

Thank You, Jesus. I know You are coming soon.

HAVEN OF REST

Dear children, let's not merely say that we love each other; let us show the truth by our actions. Our actions will show that we belong to the truth, so we will be confident when we stand before God. Even if we feel guilty, God is greater than our feelings, and he knows everything. Dear friends, if we don't feel guilty, we can come to God with bold confidence.

—*1 John 3:18–21, NLT*

I wasn't there in Escondido that day, but I could hear the relief in Dad's voice on the phone: "Nan, I stopped by Taco Bell to pick up some tostadas and suddenly realized I had left my wallet at home. The cashier took one look at me and said, 'Sir, my momma taught me how I should treat folks at times like this. There's no charge!' "

Dad assured her he would be glad to go home and bring back what he owed but the cashier insisted, "No, I've got the money right here in my purse. See, I'm taking it out right now. This one's on me!"

I sort of choked up for a moment because I knew the kindness of this young Taco Bell employee could only have come from God. My parents, both eighty-seven years old at the time, had just gone through a rough twenty-four hours and Dad just couldn't have been given a better gift at that moment!

The day before, Mom had tripped in the garden. She fractured her pelvis and was at home in bed unable to do much of anything except feel pain and begin the healing process. Dad had rushed out to get something for lunch and had forgotten his wallet. It was a little thing—but was it really?

I shared this with our church prayer meeting group later as we were studying 1 John 3. Mom's name and many other dear hearts were put on the prayer list. I couldn't forget the kind act of love at Taco Bell and felt that it was just what John was talking about when he said, "When we love others . . . we feel at ease in the presence of God, and we will have the courage to come near Him."

My duty as a daughter of God is to be alert to ways I can bless others. Some people call it "guerilla kindness"—leaving quarters in pay phones, mowing someone's lawn when they can't do it, taking the time to talk to someone who lives alone. These are deeds of the gospel of Jesus Christ—busting the stress in others' lives as well as our own. I can almost hear angels sing this beautiful old song:

"Nearer, still nearer, close to Thy heart, draw me, my Savior—so
    precious Thou art!
Fold me, oh, fold me close to Thy breast. Shelter me safe in that 'Haven
    of Rest':
Shelter me safe in that 'Haven of Rest.' " [11]

Lord, now I know how to approach You—in love for others. Then I can come boldly before You and find shelter in Your haven of rest!

FLOCK ALERT

> *"Stand up and lift up your heads, because your redemption is drawing*
> *near."*   —*Luke 21:28b, NIV*

We had just stepped off the bus at the main depot after a day of visiting
the ancient ruins of Rome, when we looked up to see a flock of birds dancing
in the sky above a grove of thickly leafed trees. Thousands of birds in black—
perhaps swallows or starlings—were moving in chorus in a tightly woven circle
forming ever-changing geometric designs in the air. The flock kept moving this
way and that and their exuberance reminded me more of a playground full of
children heading outdoors for recess than mere song birds gathering in the
sky. To my marveling soul, they seemed to be laughing, without a care in the
world, loving the energy and movement they were a part of with their feathered friends.

This symphony of movement went on for a quarter of an hour before the
tiny aviators broke for R & R to the waiting tree limbs below. Most of the pedestrians getting off work rushed on, hardly noticing the aerodynamic flock above
their heads. They just didn't look up, probably too busy with everyday things to
notice the miracle in the sky. To us, the wandering travelers, the afternoon ritual
was a reminder of God's mighty kingdom of creation offering their song of praise
to a loving heavenly Father.

I marvel even now as I sit here at my computer remembering, trying to
describe to you the beauty of symmetry and movement known as murmuration
that seemed to defy time. A couple of days later, on the other side of the globe,
a great and terrible tsunami appeared on the horizon and changed hundreds of
thousands of lives forever. Perhaps now I understand more clearly Luke's Gospel
alert: "Now when these things begin to happen, look up and lift up your heads,
because your redemption draws near" (Luke 21:28, NKJV).

HIM SINGING

> *Make a joyful noise unto the* LORD *. . . come before his presence with*
> *singing.*   —*Psalm 100:1a, 2b*

It wasn't loneliness that called me to the back stairwell of the university girls'
dorm that late Michigan evening. Quite the contrary, this was the perfect place
to sing. The acoustics were wonderful. I'd play my guitar for hours into the night,
trying to imitate the sounds of a harp. Some girls would stop by for a little while
and then leave. Others would stay and sing in harmony. I felt unashamed and
sang to my heart's content. Those were the days!

Once I visited several old Bavarian cathedrals in Germany. When most of
the visitors had gone, I tried out the acoustics. I could sing some simple hymn in

a low tone and the massive structure seemed to lift the melody high above and fill the whole cathedral with simple praise.

"Holy, holy, holy, Lord God, Almighty.

Early in the morning, my song shall rise to Thee . . ."[12]

Later that same week, I entered a castle renowned worldwide for its beauty and majesty—Ludwig's Neuschwanstein. The road up the mountain was long, even after a buggy ride halfway. I really wondered why I was trudging up this never-ending hill, when it seemed that the most famous part could be seen perfectly well from the valley below. Finally, after some breathless moments, we entered the castle gates and followed the circling steps up to the first, second, and third floors, walking through room after room of luxury and grandeur. I was impressed, but it wasn't until we entered the Throne Room that I found my reason for coming back. There, without any throne in place, was the most beautiful scene I have ever seen. Christ was depicted in a painting as King of kings high above the castle floor. Below Him were the murals of the royal line of Bavarian kings, and on each side wall were portraits of six of His apostles. I really didn't want to leave. Time seemed suspended for a moment as we stood perfectly still before the magnificent scene. These words by Reginald Heber bounced around in my heart: *"Holy, holy, holy, though darkness hide Thee, though the eye of sinful man Thy glory may not see; only Thou art holy, there is none beside Thee, perfect in power, in love and purity."*

I wished that the tour group would leave me alone in that grand room to sing to Him. I gazed at the portrait of Jesus, the King of kings, and imagined sitting at His feet and hearing Him sing me a song. Can you imagine what that would be like? One day not far from now, His voice will fill all of heaven and surround our hearts with forgiveness. Just now, I pray that together we will hold His precious feet in our hands one day and remember the walk up the hill, not the one in Germany but the one up Calvary.

DUETS

The LORD thy God, in the midst of thee is mighty; he will save, he will rejoice over thee with joy; he will rest in his love, he will joy over thee with singing.
                                                    —*Zephaniah 3:17*

I sat on the edge of my seat, casing the large indoor theater out of the corner of my eye. I was next on the program for my very first voice recital. My voice teacher figured I was ready to share my talents with the other students' parents. I was fairly confident about my voice but was getting cold feet at the thought of singing up front, especially in front of my teacher.

Then my time came. I walked up the wooden stairs hesitantly, as if each step set off another set of cannons. My feet felt like lead but my body seemed almost weightless. Out of my mouth came the first few verses of the song. I was about halfway through when, to my surprise, I noticed that my teacher was singing with me. I tried to look unaffected by this unexpected duet but inside, deep down, I was embarrassed.

How could he do that? In my teacher's quest to have everything perfect, he thought he would help me along. His voice seemed to enter my space as if he were singing a completely different song. I left that stage humbled, at the least.

I never returned to his studio for lessons. I had several voice teachers after that but my favorite encouraged me to sing what I enjoyed and showed me how to relax and enjoy the music. What a difference! One teacher led me by the ear, the other by the heart. I still sing Mr. Frey's songs. This former voice coach of Nelson Eddy showed me how to really love singing. In a way, he, too, sang with me, but we were of one heart.

My heavenly Father is like that. He sings with me. Every day I see the sunshine of His love. He releases me from fear. He laughs with me and teaches me how to rest in His love. He sings to my heart.

LIGHTS OUT!

The colorful little cog train shuddered to a stop at the entrance to the cave. Gingerly, I jumped out and joined the rest of the tour as they followed our young tour guide, Shelley, through the iron gates. A gust of underground air brushed my face with a sudden coolness, and I felt refreshed walking into the cave. But what lay ahead was not a room, but a huge web of hundreds of rooms with balconies, sunken floors, five-hundred-year-old crystal stalactites and stalagmites and intricate wave-patterned ceilings.

As we entered each new room, Shelley would turn off the room's lights and turn on the lights to a new room. Its light opened up another view of the immense underground world, bringing a whole new room to life. Without those lights, however, the room became totally black and what was indeed around us became virtually extinct.

I have always admired climbers who scale high mountains into the heavens. The adventurous explorers catch my attention, too, but I don't believe I have a desire to explore the caves in the rough. No, my comfort level requires a certain assurance that all surprises have been already discovered so that I won't fall into some deep, dark cavern or lose my way beyond the sound of anyone's voice.

This Texas cave, Inner Space, was just down the road from us. Walking on the firm ground made me feel as if I had entered another age—a kind of time warp. Every new discovery amazed me. How could such a wonderfully cool arena be beneath tumbleweeds and cacti and the sweltering Texas heat?

We were told that the cave had been accidentally discovered by highway workers some fifty years before. Excavators were checking the stability of the ground for a new highway when they realized there was a hole in the earth leading to these silent rooms. No human being had set foot there before that time. The only evidence of life was the skeletons of stray animals, which had littered the cave's floor beneath the small hole.

As we entered the last room, Shelley told us that she was going to turn off the lights and that we were to place our open hands in front of our faces and try to see our hand after the lights were out. I closed my eyes ahead of time to get them ready for the pitch blackness that quickly engulfed us. Then it was LIGHTS OUT and I couldn't see anything. It was such a strange feeling. Then we began hearing music, and a small light appeared high up on one of the rocks overflowing with crystals. The narrator began with Genesis 1:1, and the light grew larger and brighter until the whole room was bright and the reader had finished the whole Creation story. It was so beautiful and so unusual to hear the Bible quoted outside of a church.

It occurred to me that this place could have been a refuge for so many passing through the Texas desert on their way to a new home. There is quite a history of immigrant Germans journeying to Texas in search of a new home. But down in this cave where it was cool and safe, there was no ladder or way to come and go. Whatever came into this cave stayed.

God's cave of refuge is so much different. He sends His angels, as in Jacob's dream, to minister unto us, to feed us, to sustain us. It would be silly to refuse it. David, who had a lot of experience hiding in caves, said it so well:

"Rescue me and deliver me in your righteousness; turn your ear to me and save me. Be my rock of refuge, to which I can always go" (Psalm 71:2, 3a, NIV).

HOUSE SWEET HOME

I turned my head to take one last look at the house that had become our home. Everything looked so clean, so spotless, and my voice seemed to echo from bare wall to waxed floor and back again.

When I passed the base housing inspection and closed that front door for the last time, I felt I was walking out of a huge picture book and into yet another unopened book. How many times had we done this? How many times have you?

For the Troyer family, it has been almost twenty times, if we include the years in the pastorate. The places we've lived from 1970–2002 include Columbus, Georgia; Bangkok, Thailand; Berrien Springs, Michigan; Savannah, Atlanta, Macon and Thomasville, Georgia; Hixson, Tennessee; Lawton and Ft. Sill, Oklahoma; Spangdahlem AFB at Herforst, Germany; Fort Monmouth, New Jersey; Columbus, Georgia; Fort Leavenworth, Kansas; Fort Monmouth, New Jersey (second time); Seoul, South Korea; Stockbridge, Georgia; Fort Hood (Ding Dong), Texas; and Frankfurt, Germany.

Yet, when I step into a new abode for the first time, it feels so empty (no household goods, furniture, and stuff) and so lonely when we leave. The in-between is different, though. Within weeks we can transform eight hundred square feet of bare-bones living space to something so warm and familiar that we actually feel at home. You might call it "house sweet home."

I still laugh about the time when we were waiting for our household goods to arrive at Fort Monmouth. Our home was on the bottom floor of a four-apartment block building—a quadplex. There were no rugs on the floors and we went to Sears to scout out an inflatable mattress to keep us semi-comfortable. In the middle of the night, the mattress went flat and we found ourselves sleeping on a cold hardwood floor.

Tiptoeing outside, we climbed into the RV, which we took everywhere, and dragged the mattress from the queen-sized bed into the apartment. Quickly, we wrapped the precious pad in sheets and blankets. Oh, that felt so good! Soon we were off to sleep.

Since Don's retirement, I've mentally edited that phrase to read, "Home is where my heavenly Father sends me." It has helped me to realize that wherever we go, God goes before us. Whether it is in the military or civilian world, we can invite Him to lead the way.

Once we received the most beautiful picture in the mail from some friends in Korea. It shows Moses by the edge of the Red Sea with his hands raised as huge walls of water part to open a path for the Israelites to escape the Egyptians' wrath. The theme for this picture was the words of Ellen White, recited to me by Dr. Tom Geraty in 1994, just a few weeks before we left for Korea:

"The path where the Lord leads the way may go through the desert or the sea, but it is a safe place."

NOTHING MORE

One day he was praying in a certain place. When he finished, one of his disciples said, "Master, teach us to pray just as John taught his disciples." So he said, "When you pray, say, Father, Reveal who you are. Set the world right. Keep us alive with three square meals. Keep us forgiven with you and forgiving others. Keep us safe from ourselves and the Devil."
—*Luke 11:1–4, The Message*

The winds whipped around us, obscuring the fantastic view of the valley below. We were at the Eagle's Nest in southern Bavaria, huddled together under a single black umbrella in the rain. We couldn't see a thing, but our memories of previous visits helped us fill in the blanks. We figured our guest, however, didn't have that luxury, since this was his first visit to Hitler's Eagle's Nest, a summer retreat built high in the Alps. Suddenly, we noticed a break in the clouds and above us a lone black bird rode the wind currents of the departing storm. The rain vanished but the winds continued to swirl around us and the black bird kept circling above.

It was then that we were treated to a dramatic recitation of Edgar Allan Poe's "The Raven" by our guest, Barry Black, then Chief of Chaplains of the navy.

Barry was the retreat speaker for our Adventist Military Retreat, a few miles away in Garmiseh that week, and we were hosting him on a trip to our favorite city of Berchtesgaden, below us in the valley. What was so amazing besides the phenomenal view and surging storm was our guest's ability to bring to life a high school poem I gladly would have ignored in earlier years. Barry kept punctuating the ending phrases, "Nothing more . . . evermore . . . nevermore," with all the flourish of a Shakespearean actor. It was a grand event.

Later, we walked down the path around the Eagle's Nest restaurant and looked over the valley below. Don offered his cell phone to Barry, saying something like, "Wouldn't it be wonderful if the guys in your office could hear from you now?" Without hesitation, Barry grabbed the phone and called his D.C. office, chatting on and on about this and that. Meanwhile, we sat amazed at the morning's events and the mere fact that it was possible to call the States from such a lofty site.

During a recent walk with my dog Missy, I searched my memories for something to share with you. In answer to a P (for Prayer)-mail asking God to help me rustle up some thoughts, He planted the Eagle's Nest incident with Barry Black clearly in my mind. Then suddenly, like an avalanche it hit me—I was talking to the King of the universe a million miles away! I remembered a phrase from a poem: "Let my heart be still a moment and this mystery explore." I laughed deep in my soul, "Lord Jesus, You are real and You are here. I don't want to lose this revelation!"

Oh, of course, I knew this intellectually. But to roll the reality of it between my fingers stuns me into gratefulness. I desire nothing more, Lord, nothing more!

THE TABLE OF HEAVEN

Then Jesus declared, "I am the bread of life. He who comes to me will never go hungry, and he who believes in me will never be thirsty."
—John 6:35, NIV

I remember them all—Thanksgivings past, rising out of a heart far from home; a place where our extended families reside. Perhaps you recall some as well—people laughing, talking, giving thanks, eating delicious food, and communing side by side.

This was a gift-wrapped fellowship passed down through the years in faraway places such as Bangkok, Jerusalem, Spangdahlem, Frankfurt, and Seoul. I felt with family. We shared houses down the block from one another. We had empty pockets that seemed strangely full and enjoyed grand European outings to the PXs—little havens of America, far from the land of the free and the home of the brave. To be an American overseas in the military is a trip in itself.

To sit down at the table of blessing hand-in-hand with brothers and sisters of our Christian heritage, whether American, Filipino, German, Greek, Indonesian, or Ukrainian, is to sit down at the table of heaven.

Next Thanksgiving, gather together in Jesus' name. Be with us in spirit. Set a chair and a place for Him. He'll be there, too, you know. He loves to be with His children and loves to shower them with His supernatural blessings.

THE PLACE WHERE I WORSHIP

I was sitting on a log bench on the side of a hill that Sabbath day at Camp Wawona, listening to "A Church in the Wildwood." I breathed in deeply the aroma of the pine trees and studied the lush, green scenery surrounding me. What an artist God is! I was so blessed and I knew it.

If there is any place here on earth where I feel like I belong, it's summer camp—anywhere—but especially in Yosemite National Park in California. As a staff member, I could spend all summer there, eating other people's food, teaching nature classes, singing my heart out with my trusty guitar, Orlando, and rubbing shoulders with others my age who enjoyed it as much as I did. We were crazy kids, budding gypsies, living a little heaven on earth.

While there I learned another song, "The Place Where I Worship," which has continued to draw me to God and His beauty in nature through the years. A couple of months ago, I tried out the acoustics of another vacant cathedral by singing it quietly (I thought). But its music filled the air and the high and lofty arches of the aged cathedral echoed His praises in my heart.

Suzi, a friend, was listening to me sing in the cathedral. She wanted to learn the song, too, and made me promise to teach it to her when we returned to Atlanta in the fall. I didn't realize it could be special to other people. To me, it was a reminder of my time in summer camp long ago when I felt free as the breeze, ready to conquer the world in Jesus' name. But today, with the years and pounds adding up, I sing it with a deeper conviction. It isn't a song to be sung by itself. Like us, it doesn't stand alone because it is really just part of the medley that God has put in our hearts.

"Oh, the place where I worship is the wide open spaces built by the hand of the Lord,

And the trees of the forest are like pipes of an organ. The breeze plays an Amen chord.

There's a carpet of green and sky blue roof above. You can worship there alone or with the one you love.

In your heart take a good look, if you follow the Good Book, you're sure to find your reward.

Oh, the place where I worship is the wide open spaces, built by the hand of my Lord."   —Written by an anonymous cowboy

Just now, in this quiet office, I praise His name and feel so free because I know He loves me and that He loves you. He has gone away to prepare a place for us (what a place!). But, in this moment, as you read this, He is waiting beside you, whispering your name in your ear. Can you hear it? Did you know that He laughs when He says your name? Why would He do that? Because He knows you love Him and it makes Him unbelievably happy. Listen:

"I took you from the ends of the earth, from its farthest corners I called you. I said, 'You are my servant'; I have chosen you and have not rejected you. So do not fear, for I am with you; do not be dismayed, for I am your God. I will strengthen you and help you; I will uphold you with my righteous right hand" (Isaiah 41:9, 10, NIV).

OUR FIRST DATE

I've always been intrigued with dates. I remember my first date with my future husband, Don. It was a Valentine's Day party at Andrews University. But the dates I am referring to are those that repeat themselves numerically or hold some meaning in their numbers.

The most recent example of that was September 11, 2001. More emergency calls to 911 were placed that day than any other day. The date itself, when abbreviated, is 911, if you omit the slash mark.

July 7, 1977, was the first time I took note of one of these unique dates. It was 7/7/77. I remember that day very clearly. We were spending the week at a beautiful youth camp in the mountains of North Georgia, where Don was camp pastor. Even to this day, I can remember the aroma of the tall Georgia pines.

That same week, we introduced our song, "The Shout of Faith," as an altar call on Sabbath evening. Pastor Ken Rogers, a retreat speaker from the previous year, was there too. I remember God's Spirit was sweet and strong as many young hearts dedicated themselves to God. "The Shout of Faith" came flowing from my guitar in a calypsolike melody late one night during a retreat with the Atlanta Academy youth earlier that year. The words seemed so appropriate at that time.

"The Shout of Faith"
There's a lie goin' 'round that the devil can win,
We believe it and give him an in.
I believe the victory is ours.
The battle's the Lord's, His strength our power.
Shout the shout of faith with me. Sing the song of victory.
Jesus saves, He's saving me now.
Shout the shout of faith with me. Sing the song of victory.
Jesus saves. He's saving me now.

For our God is so willing this very hour.
Temptations are great, much more His power.
I believe the victory is ours.

The battle's the Lord's, His strength our power.
Shout the shout of faith with me, Jesus saves.
He's saving me now. Jesus saves. He's saving me—now!
—Don and Nancy Troyer, 1977

I know that my Savior, the God of time and space, has saved me by His precious blood. I know that He also saves me and protects me and you, this very day. When He handed out the first significant number, the seventh day of the week of Creation, He created it for our great-great-great-great-etc.-grandparents, Adam and Eve. He said to remember it. Keep our day special, always. It is, after all, our first date!

THE CROWN JEWELS

Out of the corner of my eye, I watched them curiously. Two black-cloaked women stood like silhouettes behind the Muslim gentleman. He was checking into the military hotel and looked more like the Grand Sultan than a staff sergeant in his elegant white and gold clerical robes and star-patterned knit cap crowning his head. The women, who were also American military members, looked mysterious in their *Abais,* a black dress that completely covers them, hiding even their faces.

"Now THAT is the ultimate in modesty! No one could argue with THAT," I said amusingly to myself, referring to the ongoing debate over what is adornment. I imagined myself in such a garb just for a few hours and coveted the opportunity to wear it just so I could watch others' reactions.

I've always had a bit of a pet peeve with those who considered themselves experts on the right and wrong of woman's clothing. As a lifelong Adventist, I found it easy to go without jewelry—body jewelry that is. Anything that hung from the ears, neck, wrists, fingers, or even ankles was considered taboo if it wasn't functional, like watches. Broaches and pins were in, however. Piercing adds a new twist (excuse the pun) to body jewelry.

It seems silly to me now, since I live far away from Adventist campuses and associate with Christian women who wear jewelry modestly. The most liberal thing I do now is to wear a wedding band and that only since we arrived in Germany. Actually, it felt strange, having never worn any rings all of my life.

At first I would stare at the tiny gold band and admire it. At night, however, I would take it off and breathe a sigh of relief to be un-bonded again! Ha! I'm sure all this seems really silly to those who haven't grown up in the Adventist faith.

My e-mail friend, I'll call her Mary, a conservative Mennonite, and I used to have long computer chat discussions on just this issue of jewelry. She, too, was brought up not to wear jewelry of any kind but felt it was more tradition than Bible truth. That didn't change her habits, though; she continued to go without and even wore super plain dresses and the traditional white bonnet. Her even more conservative neighbors, the Amish, would go without buttons and zippers and lace and wore dark blue or black dresses and bonnets to dress modestly.

I couldn't forget the Muslim women, however. Now THEY really seemed the essence of modesty, though not of the Christian faith. Their modesty seemed to reflect a subservient role in their society more than to avoid getting attention or giving glory to themselves, but then I didn't ask them. They certainly were getting plenty of attention at the military base where I first saw them.

Perhaps you have struggled with this issue too. On one hand I see the worthiness of not "laying up treasures on earth." But what was the apostle Paul really telling us about adornment?

He said, "Don't let your beauty be the gold braiding of hair, but the adornment of the soul." Paul brings out the Lord's jewelry and lays it on the table: the pearls of faith, the gold of joy, the diamonds of faithfulness, and the rubies of obedience. Wow! I say, if you really want to be beautiful, there really is nothing more stunning than a happy heart, adorned with the Lord's presence. This apparel is indeed the crown jewels of heaven!

THE LISTENING POST

> "Honor your father and your mother, as the LORD your God has commanded you, so that you may live long, and that it may go well with you in the land the LORD your God is giving you."
> —*Deuteronomy 5:16, NIV*

Each Father's Day I look forward to pampering the father of my child, on his day. I just hope I do a good job all by myself, as he certainly deserves it! I remember the first time we held Stephi and how I got to hold her first, completely forgetting that Don was waiting quietly over to the side just dying to hold her too.

I smile as I remember when he taught her to laugh. We were driving down Highway 1, right along the California coast, and she was wearing a cute little rainbow sleeper, giggling away at three months of age. I remember the many times I saw the two of them go out for "Dates with Dad."

One of the funniest pictures in my mind is when she got behind the wheel of our little VW Fox for her first drive. Don was sitting beside her in the passenger seat with an exaggerated picture of fright on his face.

I remember those many times when Don took the time to listen and talk with his teenager, even though he easily could have been doing something else. What a great listener and counselor he is to his beloved daughter. Whenever he returns from these little talks, he's in his "purring mode"—humming his way through the house. What a silly, sweet Dad he is. I realize, too, that not everyone is blessed with such a wonderful dad as well as a close friend. Many people out there are so very lonely because too often they have no one to listen to them.

A while back I read in "Wit & Wisdom" (Richard@witandwisdom.org) about a woman named Nancy B., who put an ad in the paper inviting troubled or lonely people to call her with problems and she would listen. I couldn't understand how she managed to do all that listening until I read that earlier, she had failed in a suicide attempt, ending up paralyzed from the waist down.

She said that while she was in the hospital, Jesus had appeared to her and told her that although she once had a healthy body and a crippled soul, from then on she would have a crippled body and a healthy soul. She accepted Christ that day and that's why she placed the listening post ad. She took the place of so many busy fathers and mothers by listening to lonely people. Nancy B., by God's grace, began to heal other souls. She was a listening post, a lighthouse in the storms of life.

Our Father in heaven loves to listen to us too. When He sent Jesus to earth, He put Him in the listening post for so many lonely souls. Right now, whether you realize it or not, He is sitting beside you, waiting to hear about your day. He doesn't get tired of listening, for after all, He died to hold you close!

P.S.: I didn't mention what a wonderful dad I have, but I do, and I love you, Dad, for all the times you listened to me!

PILLOW TALK

But thou art holy, O thou that inhabitest the praises of Israel. —Psalm 22:3

I chided myself for not finding the autumn wreath hiding somewhere in the garage. It would fit so much better than the straw couple holding a welcome home sign. After all, Steph was away at college in Germany and wouldn't be home for another seven months.

But then early one morning, I realized the sign did fit. I had been preparing for my part at the women's retreat and couldn't settle on a single idea. When asked for a title, I had casually given "Homecoming." At least it sounded good. I loved those words. Pictures of homecomings of years past filled my mind: coming out of an airport gate and seeing Mom and Dad smiling from ear to ear; landing in Thailand on an early Sabbath morning and rushing to Don's waiting arms; standing in a crowded bus terminal on Christmas Eve searching among the throng for our returning Airman Steph. Each involved big hugs and happy hearts. It is always good to be home where your heart is.

Years ago at Fort Leavenworth, I wrote a song entitled "Home in Your Heart," referring to a scripture verse that said in so many words that God loves to dwell in the praises of His people. That was the verse I needed right then for my presentation, but I couldn't find it until I awoke that morning and the word *inhabit* popped into my head. I had searched the Internet in vain until my pillow epiphany. The word *inhabit* was like a beacon of hope and cheer—an audible "Hello!" from God— "He inhabits the praises of His people."

I quickly copied the text and went back to bed, but I couldn't sleep. I prayed earnestly to get a few more winks before rising, but mental pictures kept popping up: Jesus and me huddled in a blanket; taking an early morning walk in the neighborhood; chopping onions in the kitchen; behind the wheel of my car, driving to physical therapy; alone together in the house, kneeling in prayer. And then it became clear to me: the sign on the door was for Jesus!

I was welcoming Jesus home—home in my heart. Right there on my pillow, He was telling me how to open the door to my heart: *"I will inhabit, dwell, be literally beside you, when you sing songs of praise to Me. But not just in song; also in every thank You and audible prayer, and even on paper by pen in your praise journal."*

Remember for a moment the times in your life when you have felt Him near—perhaps during a beautiful song. Those priceless moments strengthen you and give you a glimpse of the heavenly homecoming. Let Him come home to your heart now through your words of thanksgiving. He never misses a reunion!

Welcome home, Jesus!

THE OUTER WALL

I awoke to a quiet golden morning and peeked outside to view the sand-colored housetops bunched together all over Jerusalem. The sun was just beginning to warm the air that long-ago November. We had been traveling around Israel for almost a week and finally had landed at the King David Hotel in Jerusalem for the night. I felt like I was in a dream, but awoke rather abruptly when I smelled the fishy lox ready for our breakfast bagels in the dining room. We set out that day to walk the streets where Jesus walked.

After several blocks of rough cobblestone streets and noisy crowds, we turned a corner and gazed at a huge wall looming in front of us. It was the West Wall of Old Jerusalem—preserved and revered for centuries. In the distance, I could hear a strange high-pitched staccato melody which spoke of its other name, the Wailing Wall. A twelve-year-old Israeli boy was coming of age and the mothers of Israel were both lamenting and celebrating beside their sacred wall. There was a men's section and a women's section, so Chaplain Don went off with the bearded, skull-capped throng and I stood still taking in the whole scene.

There was only a sprinkling of women approaching our side of the wall. Beside me in a basket lay small slips of paper. A sign said they were for prayers that would be placed in the wall. I took one and walked over to the huge chunks of sandy-colored brick still neatly stacked generations later. I rubbed my hand on the famous wall and looked straight up into a cloudless sky. Everything seemed so silent. Finally, I knew whose names I would insert into the wall, not so much as a prayer for them but for a thank You to God for their lives.

The tears started to roll down my face and strangely the sounds of wailing returned and I felt cleansed and relaxed. I turned to leave the women's area deep in thought, looking back once more to take a mental snapshot of the scene. Then these words from Revelation 21 describing another wall came flooding into my heart:

"I saw Holy Jerusalem, new-created, descending resplendent out of Heaven, as ready for God as a bride for her husband. I heard a voice thunder from the Throne: 'Look! Look! God has moved into the neighborhood, making His home with men and women! They're his people, he's their God. He'll wipe every tear from their eyes. Death is gone for good. . . . The City shimmered like a precious gem, light-filled, pulsing light. She had a wall majestic and high with twelve gates. . . . The wall was jasper, the color of Glory, and the City was pure gold, translucent as glass. . . . But there was no sign of the Temple, for the Lord God . . . and the Lamb are the Temple. The City doesn't need sun or moon for light. God's Glory is its light, the Lamb its lamp!" (excerpts from Revelation 21, The Message).

I close my eyes and see!

SNOW MOON

"For where two or three come together in my name, there am I with them."
—*Matthew 18:20, NIV*

I turned over in my bed in the rustic motel cabin to peek outside. The air was crisp and fresh, the room was bright with morning light. Had I overslept? No, we were on our "first honeymoon." I relaxed. There was no need to rush off to work or meet any deadlines this day.

I stopped a moment to realize where we were. We were nestled deep in the property of Callaway Gardens. What was that falling from the forest trees? SNOW? Not in South Georgia! I jumped out of bed to take a closer look.

"Don, it's snowing!" I yelled in excitement and danced from window to window examining the landscape. Outside was a winter wonderland. Everything from trees to cars to grass to rooftops was covered in a thick layer of fresh snow—unbelievable, especially considering that yesterday when we arrived the whole area was green and lush with Southern hospitality and the scent of Georgia pines.

Later, when we ventured out for a drive around the park to find a place to eat, we realized we were the only ones in the park, except for the staff in the lodge. Callaway Gardens was ours!

We ate like kings and marveled at the winter wonderland outside. This was, after all, our first wedding anniversary, Honeymoon #1, and Valentine's Day wrapped into one. You might call it our "Snow Moon"—a rare and beautiful phenomenon—the silver light of hope!

Since then, we have celebrated many "honeymoons." Each anniversary is better than the last. Each one is a celebration of the love God has given us. We know we couldn't have made it all these years on our own—nobody can. There have been good days and bad. Boring days—no, I can't say that; never boring. Our life together has been one great conversation. Sometimes we banter, other times we tease each other or just talk for hours about everything under the moon.

Then there are the moments of angered silence that seem to suck the oxygen out of the room. Sometimes we ask forgiveness and the air grows light again. But you know what? One thing I know for sure is that Jesus is always with us on our journey. How do I know that? Because in Matthew 18:20, He said, "When two or three of you are together because of me, you can be sure that I'll be there" (The Message).

So maybe He's just the referee, or the cheerleader, or the counselor, the shepherd, the lamplight on a darkened night. Maybe He is the waiter in the white coat who cleans the table and quietly picks up the money for our tab.

Does that sound too common? Not to me. That's what Jesus does best—being common, being one of us, to bring us together in holy, heavenly love. All we have to do is ask.

After all, He loves to hear His Name!

THE HEAVENLY TIME KEEPER

And we know that all things work together for good to them that love God, to them who are the called according to his purpose. —Romans 8:28

She stood before me extending her hand as we filed out of church that autumn afternoon in 1974. As I took her hand to thank her for her testimony, I was surprised at her large frame. She wasn't fat, just bigger than I, yet the words of her testimony made her seem fragile and sweet and dependent. Physically, however, she did not appear to be any of those things.

I had never heard her name before, yet everyone else seemed so excited about this elderly daughter of a Dutch watchmaker. "Corrie ten Boom is the author of *The Hiding Place*," they told me. "What is that?" I asked, somewhat irritated that I had definitely missed something that was important, to the others, at least.

What I remember about that evening at the Downers Grove Adventist Church sundown vespers was the illustration she used. She held up a piece of cloth. "This is your life," she said. "At least, this is the way you see your life." She had held up the back side of a piece of cross-stitch. The back side looked pretty messy, all right. Then she turned the cloth around to reveal a beautifully crafted cross-stitched crown. "But this is how God sees your life," she announced triumphantly. "You are His crown, you are His masterpiece. You are beautiful."

A few weeks later, I purchased a copy of *The Hiding Place* and learned about her experiences in a World War II concentration camp.

The following year, Don and I were in Illinois when we received a call from my father. "Please sit down," Dad said over the phone. My pulse raced and then he spoke words that no one wants to hear: "Your brother Steve and Sharilyn have been killed in a car accident."

I struggled to grasp the message. Just ten days previously, we had driven from Andrews University out to Lincoln, Nebraska, to attend their wedding. In a fog of sorrow later that afternoon, I remember going outside and sitting alone under a tree with our little Schnauzer Fritzy. I hugged him and cried, "How could this happen, Lord? And for that matter, why? They were so young, just beginning their lives together."

In a few days, we flew back to Nebraska to attend their funeral in the same church where they were married. My whole body trembled. This was my little brother. "God, I don't understand!"

Later, back at home, I was sent another copy of *The Hiding Place*. But this one held special significance. It was the one found on the floor of Steve and Sharilyn's little green Volkswagen. *Perhaps,* I thought to myself, *Sharilyn was reading this book as they were coming back from their honeymoon.*

I paged through its chapters aimlessly, until I noticed something odd. The top edge of the pages in the second half of the book were torn off. I opened to where the torn section began and started reading at this passage:

> "Daddy," little Corrie asked. "I need you . . . You can't just die!" Her father sat down beside her bed and asked her a question, "When we go to Amsterdam, when do I buy you a ticket?" Little Corrie answered quickly, "Why, when we get on the train." Her father continued, "Exactly, and our wise Heavenly Father knows when we're going to need things, too. Don't run out ahead of Him, Corrie. When the time comes that some of us will have to die, you will look into your heart and find the strength you need, just in time."

I sat there stunned with the book in my hands. Had Sharilyn been holding this book just as the accident happened? I didn't know. But what I did know was that the message was for me too. God was comforting me: *"Nancy, I know you have a broken heart; I am here right now in your darkest hour."*

During those dark days after I lost my baby brother, I experienced the wonderful gift of God's golden presence. Yes, I grieved, but not like I would have ordinarily because I knew that God was right beside me.

Some of you have experienced sadness in your lives. You have lost loved ones unexpectedly and probably feel quite empty sometimes. Remember this: God doesn't miss anything in our lives. He is eager to give us strength just when we need it most, and I believe this too. He cries with us and one day will make all things beautiful. This chorus says it so well:

"In His time, in His time, He makes all things beautiful in His time.
Lord, please show me everyday as You're teaching me Your way,
That You do just what You say, in Your time."[13]

Thank you, heavenly Time Keeper. We wait for Your soon coming. Amen!

Notes on . . .
The Sufficiency of God's Grace

In Depression and Grief
In Tragedy
In Times of Conflict

In Awkward Situations
When We Need Protection
In Times of Weakness

YOU DON'T WALK AWAY . . .

The first time I met Jean, I recoiled at the sound of her voice. She was using a microphone held closely to her throat in order to burp up the sounds of words and phrases she wanted to share with her friends. The sound was loud and monotone. I made an excuse to leave the room.

I had been working at the Rosewood, a senior citizen home in Texas, for only a few days at that time. In the weeks that followed, I went about my duties driving residents to shopping malls, bingo parlors, and doctors' visits. Slowly, I began to love this tiny lady with the big smile, who just happened to use a microphone. She was always positive and so refreshing and encouraging that I no longer heard the monotone in her voice. I could see a smile in her eyes.

Sometimes the residents would ask me to take them somewhere personal, like the time Jean asked me to drive her to the cemetery. Her husband's crypt was there and she said she was just lonely for him.

I jumped at the chance to get to know her better. She had been a smoker all her life and had quit just a couple of years before her throat cancer was discovered. She lost her voice. Some people never come out of this dark hole of depression and grief. They just give up and walk away. But Jean loved life and people too much and fought to regain her voice. The microphone and Jean were constant companions and she didn't miss a chance to speak up.

When we arrived at the cemetery chapel, I opened the door for Jean and planned to wait quietly for her by the car. But Jean insisted that I also come in. We walked into the chapel and then I busied myself across the room to give her some privacy. I could hear no sound from Jean (she wasn't using her microphone now), but I could tell she was crying. Tears also welled up in my heart.

So many things had changed for this remarkably independent woman— cancer, the loss of her voice, her husband's death, moving to a single room in a group home, and the impending sale of her beloved house. The Rosewood was a beautiful place. I had often joked that if they would just buy a limousine, the home would be complete. But it wasn't home; it couldn't be.

Jean motioned for me to come closer and I winked a smile as I followed her to the beautiful marble square on the wall in memory of her husband. I could tell the love they shared was not dead. I asked if I could pray for her and she lightly laughed, quickly bowed her head, and closed her eyes with the microphone in her lap. "Dear Jesus," I said, "thank You for Jean."

The warm look she gave me as I dropped her off later that day at the back door near her room was special. I felt so rich and certainly blessed just to know her. I knew Jesus loved Jean and I prayed that one day in heaven I would be able to hear her real voice. I knew it would be as beautiful as her smile. I thought of the Divine Healer as I read these words from Colossians 1: "He was supreme in the beginning and—leading the resurrection parade—he is supreme in the end. From beginning to end he's there, towering far above everything, everyone. So spacious is he, so roomy, that everything of God finds its proper place in him without crowding. Not only that, but all the broken and dislocated pieces of the universe—people and things, animals and atoms—get properly fixed and fit together in vibrant harmonies, all because of his death, his blood that poured down from the cross. . . . You don't walk away from a gift like that! . . . There is no other Message—just this one" (verses 18–23, The Message).

THE LIVING WATER

One of the great things about living in Europe is the opportunity to visit places others only read about. There was an occasion when we traveled by tour bus to Italy. The bus ride was wonderful and terrible at the same time. For instance, I didn't have to drive and, oh, my aching body! But when we stopped and surveyed the precious monuments of this earth, from Pisa's leaning tower, Florence's *David,* Pompeii's pillared square, Capri's seaside gardens, and Rome's majestic palaces to Venice's silent canals, I couldn't shake the thought that every place had precious people woven like fine gold into the fabric of its everyday life.

Of all the many wonderful sights, one simple object caught my attention—a short, hollowed-out Roman column in one of Pompeii's courtyard gardens. I had never seen a well like this, so tiny yet so useful. It was just a bucket lowered into the hollowed-out marble column deep into the earth, which brought its owners the cherished fresh water they needed.

This city was alive and active when Christ was walking the paths of Palestine. But these people didn't know the Living Water, Jesus Christ. They cherished the water of the earth, the colors of the seas, and passion itself. All of these things vanished with one giant volcanic eruption.

You hear about the thousands who perished, their agony preserved by volcanic cinders for our wondering eyes to observe. But what about the other eighteen thousand who escaped, leaving their slaves behind?

I just wonder—where did they go? Did they make their way to places where Christ or His friends would one day meet them later in life? Did they taste of the

Water of Life? Did they find Someone and something they could keep forever? Out of all that tragedy and chaos, did even one of them end up at the feet of Jesus?

I keep remembering the feel of the fine angular marble edges of that Roman well under my fingers, and the hot sultry morning when I walked along the streets of Pompeii. I believe that sometimes the worst of life brings us unknowingly to the River of Blessing, the Water of Life, the Forever.

Dear Father, in these troubled times, open our eyes to the place we are right now. Let us smell the sweet alabaster of Your grace, taste the sweet kindness of the Water of Life, and hold tightly onto Your all encompassing arms. Let us laugh with joy at Your goodness, cherish the eternal and trace with our fingers the precious steps of the Almighty. Amen.

A BRIDGE CALLED FAITHFUL

Shout for joy to the LORD, all the earth. Worship the LORD with gladness; come before him with joyful songs. Know that the LORD is God. It is he who made us, and we are his; we are his people, the sheep of his pasture. Enter his gates with thanksgiving and his courts with praise; give thanks to him and praise his name. For the LORD is good and his love endures forever; his faithfulness continues through all generations. —Psalm 100, NIV

The first time I met Don's mother I was being led blindly through the back roads of northern Indiana to an all-night Gospel Sing. It was our second date and the intriguing young college student who had invited me to this musical extravaganza neglected to mention that his mother would be coming along. As we came up the driveway, Irene came bounding out of the house, obviously happy to be going with us. *Oh, well,* I thought, *at least he likes his mother!*

At the concert, I sat between them. We marveled at the melodious sounds coming from the stage far below our lofty position in the balcony. Between beautiful praises to God, laughter and goodwill filled the evening. This was really fun—enjoying a date with someone's mother! I wondered how the girls back at the dorm would react when I told them. Before the evening was over, however, my skepticism was put to rest when a remarkable new song was introduced. The timeless melody of "Danny Boy" and the angel-like song composed by Dottie Rambo touched my soul deeply.

"Amazing grace shall always be my song of praise, for it was grace that
    bought my liberty.
I do not know just why Christ came to love me so. He looked beyond my
    fault and saw my need.
I shall forever lift my eyes to Calvary to view the cross where Jesus died for
    me.
How marvelous the grace that caught my falling soul. He looked beyond my
    fault and saw my need."[14]

Wow! Even when I felt invincible, high on life and without a pang of want or need back there in my twenties, God whispered to me reminding me of His amazing grace. Thank You, Jesus!

At Thanksgiving I remember the goodness of God who provided me with a wonderful husband, a precious daughter, and an attentive mother-in-law who loved music as much as she did her sons. "For the LORD is good and his love endures forever; his faithfulness continues through all generations."

CHRISTIAN ROCK

At the Rhein Main Lodging in Frankfurt, Germany, where I worked as registration clerk, I was talking to a couple of former servicemen about their years in the military.

An old career veteran, Harry, requested two adjoining rooms for his wife and himself. Slightly embarrassed, Harry whispered to me that he had sleep problems and it was best for each of them if they slept in separate beds. "Ever since Vietnam, I sleep very restlessly," he said, "flailing my arms and such throughout the night." I agreed with him that it was a good thing we had the extra room.

Later, I shared Harry's story with Jim, a coworker, who confided that he also was in Vietnam, but since the war he just curls up in a little ball and has no problem sleeping anymore. I asked Jim about his experiences and he said that he couldn't talk about it except to say that it was only by the grace of God that he was alive today. There were too many close calls during his three years in Vietnam for him to come to any other conclusion but that God was by his side all through that terrible conflict.

I thought about Harry and Jim. Both had experienced a lot of trauma during their days in Vietnam, and yet each came away with an entirely different set of emotional baggage. Harry never mentioned God and I'm not sure where he stood with the Lord. Jim simply stated that he knew God had blessed him and spared him for some special purpose in life. Harry slept fitfully and Jim slept like a baby.

That reminds me of an old Negro spiritual: "Rock-a my soul in the bosom of Abraham, Rock-a my soul in the bosom of Abraham, Rock-a my soul in the bosom of Abraham. Oh, Rock-a my soul . . ."

As you hit the pillow tonight, ask God to rock you to sleep. Then fall back in His arms and close your eyes. You're safe, you know. That's great Christian Rock!

GLOVES

"I have loved you with an everlasting love; I have drawn you with loving-kindness."
—Jeremiah 31:3, NIV

I opened the large package with eager hands to see what my folks had sent this time. One of the items seemed curious to me—inside were two pairs of hunting gloves from Wal-Mart. I am not a hunter. Neither is Don. But the feel of the soft jersey material brought back a flood of memories of other gloves in my past.

My first gloves, as I recall, were for my Lynwood Academy senior banquet—a pair of full-length formal white gloves—going all the way to my elbows. Later, I remember Mrs. Bonifay, our battalion commander's wife, telling us what she had to go through to present herself as a good officer's wife—from hats to shoes and gloves too. Fortunately, she was not asking us to follow suit. Those rules belonged to another era of military social graces.

My most treasured gloves were a pair of leather ones that I received one Texas Christmas from my beloveds, Don and Steph. I had barely taken them out of their lovely holiday wrapping, when I absentmindedly dropped them in the parking lot as I exited our car. Someone else felt they were a gift from above because the gloves were gone when we returned to our car.

The last time I sent someone else gloves was when my cousin asked us all to send gloves to share with the poor village people in the Muslim country where they were missionaries. Gloves as witnesses? That request changed my perspective on gloves.

Gloves, after all, are so comforting since they provide warmth to one of the most sensitive areas of our body. You would think everyone would wear them in winter—but there are a few unique individuals who would rather risk frostbite than be inconvenienced by wearing them.

Gloves are meant to protect and comfort. If you look closely at the word *gloves,* you see that it *almost* spells G-Loves, or God Loves. God loves to protect us by covering us with His kindnesses. Sometimes He sends His gifts of kindness before we ask, like the gloves my parents sent. Other times, He waits for us to ask, to feel our need of His protection.

I'm looking at my hands right now, asking God to cover them with His gloves of grace.

"Lord Jesus, place Your kindness in my hands, so that I may be aware of others in need, whether it be a physical need, emotional healing, or a spiritual sister-hug. God, You promised us just this. So, Lord, I ask that Your gilt of perception clasped with my response of gratefulness will open my weary eyes to others' needs. This Thanksgiving as we sit down to the table of abundance, I want to thank You for Your everlasting kindness that is sweeter than honey. I remember Your gloveless hands, scarred for eternity with the nail prints of the cross and, Lord, I want to see Your hands. Amen!"

HE KNOWS YOUR NAME!

"Fear not, for I have redeemed you; I have summoned you by name; you are mine."
—Isaiah 43:1b, NIV

The moist green grass refreshed my hot bare feet that Fourth of July, far away from home, in 1972. I remember admiring the huge flag that was waving over the American Embassy in Thailand. That flag looked so good to this American expatriate. It felt like I was home again. I remember wiping tears from my eyes as I listened to the band play many familiar songs: "This Land Is Your Land," "God Bless America," "Yankee Doodle," "America the Beautiful," "Dixie," "The Green Beret."

These things—the Flag and the songs—hadn't seemed that special to me back in the States, but after a year in this Asian country, so close to the war zone of Vietnam, they were precious to me. Thailand was a wonderful place—sunny days, set-your-clock afternoon rains, abundant fruit and flower leis, five-star restaurants at bargain prices, colorful silk cloth, and last but not least, an Adventist church family to worship with.

The Thai people were friendly and warm and although we were a struggling enlisted military family, we could easily afford a house full of furniture for what it would cost to buy one sofa now—rattan and teak furniture that we still have in our home today. Even with all Thailand had to offer, my heart felt warmed sitting and absorbing something familiar from my motherland.

Our fourth floor apartment was just down the street from the converted bowling alley then serving as the Protestant/Catholic/Jewish U.S. military chapel where Don worked. He was a chaplain's assistant back then, supporting chaplains as they ministered to the military community. The apartment we lived in was situated on the Klong River that ran through Bangkok. Sometimes I would step onto the balcony to enjoy the wonderful tropical aromas of balmy nights and sunny days filled with fruit and flowers.

One day, I remember watching my landlady next door step outside carrying a bowl of fruit and incense. She carefully placed the fruit around the minia-ture temple house, which was standing at eye level on a pole in her backyard. Then she lighted the incense, bowing respectfully at what she believed to be her deceased ancestor's spirit abode. The gold leaf trim sparkled in the warm tropical sun as she turned to leave.

Another day I spotted a Buddhist monk in orange saffron robes stopping at the front door to receive his daily offering of rice. All these things were important to this family because by doing these deeds they felt they could obtain salvation and safety and goodwill for the "next life." If they were lucky—and luck would always play a role in their minds—after death they just might make it to the next rung on the ladder to paradise: for men, perhaps coming back as an elephant; for women, coming back as a man. If they were bad, uncaring, or ignored their reli-gious rituals, they believed they might end up in the "next life" coming back as a dog, or even worse, as a cockroach.

I watched all this and realized how blessed I was to grow up in a Christian family knowing from my earliest years that my salvation wasn't dependent on my good works at all but on the death of Jesus Christ on the cross. I already knew I didn't have to pacify the gods to advance in the next life. I knew that Jesus was my Savior. In fact, He is the One who took my place, my punishment. If I am willing to open the door to Him and let Him into my heart, I am covered with His goodness and free forever. "Nancy," He says, "I'm here; may I come in?" He knows your name, too, and loves to say it out loud. Listen—you can hear Him.

SNAPSHOTS OF GRACE

"And so I tell you, keep on asking, and you will receive what you ask for. Keep on looking, and you will find. Keep on knocking, and the door will be opened to you."   —Luke 11:9, NLT

It was the end to a special weekend. Reluctantly, my two friends and I gathered our belongings together and headed to the car. Once inside, we debated about which outlet mall to visit before we took the big trip back to Atlanta and our busy homes. Our choice became simple when we realized the closest one hadn't opened yet. We headed south on the highway, holding onto the fading memories of the women's convention: Bright costumes, unfamiliar languages, soulful songs, rippling laughter, easy tears, and sometimes, true confessions.

During most of the meetings, we sat in the shadows because the lights weren't working well. It was a strange sensation not to see the facial expressions of the women sitting nearby, but it helped me focus on Carla Gober, our speaker, who definitely knew how to express the many things in her heart. Yes, she was a professional, but at the same time a sister, a reflection of the many crazy friends I have acquired through the years.

Ah, there it was! We turned off the highway and began looking for a place to get some sodas before we began pounding the sidewalks in the mall. We discovered most of the fast-food places were still closed. Our zigzag journey brought us to one far down the street that was open. Relieved to finally find our watering hole, Suzi ordered the drinks with a little tease in her voice. I laughed from the backseat figuring the attendant might be smiling too. We drove up to the window to pay the bill but were surprised to hear, "No charge!" A pregnant pause filled the air "What?" Marsha and I chimed in a bit quieter than Suzi's amazed response. "How much?" she asked. "No charge," the attendant repeated, adding, "My manager said, 'Don't charge 'em!' " Our mouths fell open. "Th-th-*thaaank* you," Suzi spoke haltingly for us all.

We laughed as she sped out of the parking lot, hardly believing our good fortune. In the back seat, in the shadows again, I mulled over the last moment's event. I held no free drink in my hands but I felt blessed just to witness the kindness of a stranger. The fading convention memories took on a new perspective to me. We had listened as it was explained to us how to live in the "middle" of our lives—without a past or future possessing us—resting in God's will, listening for His voice. In this simple act of kindness I found His voice speaking to me, echoing His grace, *"Ask Me, Nancy, and I will give you . . . look and I will show you*

. . . don't give up your dreams; make Me a part of them!"

GRANDMA'S QUILT

"For I know the plans I have for you," declares the LORD, "plans to prosper you and not to harm you, plans to give you hope and a future. Then you will call upon me and come and pray to me, and I will listen to you. You will seek me and find me when you seek me with all your heart.
—*Jeremiah 29:11–13, NIV*

"Grandma, when you die, can I have that nice statue in the corner?"

I can't believe I said that to my grandma, but I did back when I was little. And of course, you want to ask, "Did you get the statue?"

No, I'm sad to say, I didn't, but I did get something very special from my grandmother. She loved to sew and often on birthdays she would give me one of her handmade flowery-print aprons.

Grandma was a great cook, too, and in her kitchen, so immaculately clean and white, we would always find her making something special, from German kuchen (fruit pies) to unique anise-flavored cookies called Springerle. I still have her special wooden rolling pin passed down to me by my mom, who was her daughter-in-law.

Years later after Grandma died all of her granddaughters were given one of her beautiful quilts. There were several of us girls so making a quilt for each of us was no small task, especially considering that Grandma died in her early seventies just when life was slowing down for her.

What was so precious about my quilt was that it was made from the same flowery fabrics she had used in all the different aprons she had given me over the years. I treasure Grandma's quilt and still have it to this day even though it is now a bit fragile from use and age. You see, I didn't pack it away like fine china but I used it, spreading it on my bed, hanging it in the corner, or just cuddling up in its surprising warmth.

Jesus said that He wouldn't abandon us if we call on Him with all our heart. He knows what He's doing; He has it all planned out! Right now, I'm smiling inside as I think about Jesus. Over the years, the precious Son of God has been giving us beautiful gifts.

This I know with certainty, for He has given me the gift of a wonderful family, both in my childhood and present life. He has given me friends who are near and dear to my heart, even though some of them live far away. He has given me talents and memories and so much more that I probably am not even aware of.

I know that when I get to heaven, Jesus is going to wipe away the tears from my eyes so I can see His master plan; so I can see the whole picture of why things happened the way they did.

I think it will be as beautiful and full of memories as my grandma's quilt!

CHANGING COMMAND

And he said unto me, My grace is sufficient for thee: for my strength is made perfect in weakness. Most gladly therefore will I rather glory in my infirmities, that the power of Christ may rest upon me.
— 2 *Corinthians 12:9*

I remember the first day I met her. She seemed so shy and quiet, yet very much aware of her surroundings. We rode in the van together back to Atlanta and then the Day family placed her in our arms, barely three days old. Ted was a fine Christian lawyer we first met in Thomasville, Georgia, where we built our first home and had our first church family. God moved Ted and his family to just the right location to help us when we needed it to adopt our baby in a state where private adoptions were discouraged.

Although Stephanie is not bone of my bone, she is definitely heart of my heart, our hearts. Don and I had been married for twelve years before God placed Stephanie in our hearts. That is how it all started. We were quite content as just a couple, we thought. But God started working on our hearts almost to the day of her conception, preparing us for that phone call that would change our lives. If we could go back in time, had the choice to change our decision, to avoid the pain and the big and little things that parents struggle with, would we do that? No way. God has blessed us with so much love, so much insight and deep commitment for Him and for Stephanie, our child.

In May of 2002, Stephanie, then just past twenty, headed out on her own. She joined Uncle Sam in the United States Air Force and entered a new phase in her life. As parents, we know her weaknesses and struggles, but God knows her better than we do and He has assured me that He will never leave her. If I had one prayer, one request to God for my Steph, it would be that wherever she goes she will be free—to laugh, to build on failures as well as successes, to love God without hesitation, to walk in His steps, and to hang on to His power in her heart—free, indeed!

I'm going to cry a bit now and then for a while, but that's OK. I'm going to imagine myself as a little mouse tucked precariously in her backpack. I was thinking of her the times she stepped on the plane looking back on her beloved Germany and as she walked up the corridor into the Texas heat and the land of the Big Sky. I could imagine myself as that silly little mouse sitting in her pocket, nose up trying to catch a breath of fresh air and a view of the outside world as she checked into the barracks and ate her first three-minute meal.

I wonder what she was thinking when the first sergeant told her he was her mother. I wish I could have been sitting on the grass, water glass in hand, when she got side aches from muscling her way through the obstacle course. I would like to have been in her pocket next to her heart in a way, checking it all out. Well, I wish I could have done this, but I found a good substitute mother to do all that. He held her first, before me, before anyone in this world held her. He touched her heart the first time it struck a beat, a note in time. His name is Jesus.

JUST BORROWED

Every animal of the forest is already mine. The cattle on a thousand hills are mine. I know every bird on the mountains, and every living thing in the fields is mine.   —Psalm 50:10, 11, NCV

It was the summer of 1995 and we had received military orders to move to Fort Hood, Texas. We were living in Georgia, just south of Atlanta at the time. The day was hot and humid, and far above our comfort level. The packers' van pulled into our driveway and out jumped several workers carrying a load of cardboard boxes to fill.

This was certainly going to be a full day, I thought to myself, with packers everywhere plus a farewell luncheon to go to. I called our neighbor and asked if she would be willing to "house sit" while we were away. She agreed to help us out.

Soon the house was filled with the sound of packing tape. Back in those days we had the luxury of having all of our belongings packed for us. We didn't mind strangers handling our things but kept a watchful eye just to keep them honest. We were the fortunate ones. We had never lost anything and had come to trust these hard workers who had made our gypsy life simpler.

But this morning as I sat watching the flurry of activity, I heard a loud crashing sound in the kitchen. I rushed to see what had happened and observed a packer tossing metal cookie sheets into a big box as fast as he could. I mustered up a joking tone of voice and told him to be more careful with my things. To my surprise, the man retorted, "I've been doing this job for ten years, ma'am, and I don't need anyone telling me how to do it!"

I was surprised by his blunt remark and left the room to ease the tension. Later, I returned to a quieter kitchen and saw one of our treasures leaning against a wall waiting to be packed. It was a silk screen displaying hand-stitched pandas. I had found it in Korea and loved it. It certainly was one of the most beautiful items in our home. I wondered where I should put it in our next place.

Before we knew it, our home was emptied of all our possessions and a for-sale sign graced the lawn. This place we had known as our home was just a house again with only the lonely echo of our voices bouncing off the bare walls.

When our household goods arrived in Texas and we opened box after box, I noticed that my panda screen was nowhere to be found. I called the moving company to check whether it might have been left on the truck but they hadn't heard anything about it.

As I scanned the inventory and noticed there was no mention of our treasure, I remembered that the kitchen packer hadn't shown up the next day to help load the truck and I began to piece together what might have happened.

There had been a large stack of flattened boxes to be taped up in the same room where my panda silk screen had been leaning against a wall. It would have been a real temptation for someone who saw the lovely screen just to slip it between the sheets of cardboard and carry it to the packers' van at the end of that first day.

As I thought about that scenario, I realized that it had been stolen right from under my nose. My trusting spirit began to crumble as I imagined the packer proudly showing it to a pawnshop owner.

One day while grieving the loss, I stopped long enough to listen to God. *"Nan,"* He said, *"what are you doing? You have been blessed in so many ways. The material things I have given to you for just a little while. Be thankful you have had them and let them go, for 'where your treasure is, there will your heart be also.'"* He continued with a smile in His voice, *"You know, Nan, these things are just borrowed from Me, for everything belongs to Me! I own the cattle on a thousand hills; I own your savings; I own everything you hold dear. Learn to cherish only those things that last forever!"*

HUGGED BY THE STARS

> *When I consider thy heavens, the work of thy fingers, the moon and the stars, which thou hast ordained; what is man, that thou art mindful of him? and the son of man, that thou visitest him? For thou hast made him a little lower than the angels, and hast crowned him with glory and honour.* —Psalm 8:3–5

I have to confess, I am a closet camper. I dream of days gone by in the Path-finders youth group when I would scramble up mountains and hug trees. The aroma of pine trees and the rustle of leaves beneath my feet still bring music to my ears.

I spent two summers on staff at Camp Wawona, an Adventist summer camp just north of Yosemite National Park in California. I learned a lot about rocks and ferns because I was drafted to teach these subjects to admiring campers. I fine-tuned my guitar and could sing just about any campfire song, even in my sleep! But the greatest campout I ever experienced was not spent in the depths of a national forest or in the far reaches of a desert floor.

It was my freshman year at Pacific Union College in Northern California. I suppose life must have been getting dull up on Howell Mountain because a few of us girls began to ponder life "outside the box."

As everything quieted down around campus, my friends and I silently lugged our bedding up the seldom-used stairs to the roof of the senior girls' dorm. Silence soon enveloped sleepy conversations and shortly after midnight we settled down in our beds. Then in the quiet I began focusing on a majestic ocean of stars above me. I felt so small—like a miniature me in a storybook. I tried to look beyond the stars and talked quietly in my head to God. *Wow, Jesus, this is all Yours? And You still are interested in me? Why?*

In the back of my mind, an old memory began to emerge—Mom playing the piano and singing the words to a psalm: *"When I consider thy heavens, the work of thy fingers, the moon and the stars, which thou hast ordained, what is man that thou art mindful of him?"*

The lullaby danced in my head and suddenly I felt so precious, like a child enfolded in her father's arms. *"Thou hast made him a little lower than the angels, and hast crowned him with glory and honour."* Tears formed in the corners of my upturned eyes. "Why would I ever want to go to sleep?" I mused. But I relaxed and fell asleep in the sweet peace of His amazing grace.

Notes on . . .
Expressing Gratitude and Praise to God

For Our Freedoms
For Christian Friends and Family
For God's Provisions
For the Good News of the Gospel

SHARE THE GOOD NEWS

"No one lights a lamp and then puts it under a basket. Instead, a lamp is placed on a stand where it gives light to everyone in the house."
—Matthew 5:15, NLT

From My Diary:

It's 10 P.M. Thanksgiving Eve and the Servicemen's Center air is full of the aroma of cinnamon and apples. I am glad to be settling down and taking time to organize for tomorrow's activities. I'm also glad to be off work from my job as reservation clerk at Rhein Main Lodging and to put that behind me until next week.

Yesterday was a truly stressful day. I learned a lesson on listening and passing on news. In my quest to be a perfect employee, I forgot the most important thing about being part of a team: keeping others informed on new situations.

An air crew came in and had to spend more time in front of our counter than they wanted and you probably can guess the rest of the story. There were complaints and chastisements all the way up the chain of command.

I thought to myself that there must be some good lesson here for me—something I could carry into my spiritual life. I mean it soothes a guilty conscience when one can create a life lesson from a fall from grace, right? So I thought for a while and realized that this must be how God feels when He bestows the good news of the gospel on our hearts and we cherish it but don't pass it on.

After all, the good news is not really good news until it's passed on. The good news that Jesus gives us is all about freedom. He tells me that I can be free, freer than I ever thought or dreamed, by taking time to get to know Him. I've told my daughter many times that if there is just one thing in life I could give her it would be freedom. Some of the most powerful Christians I know have been able to pass on His freedom through their spirit of gratitude and praise. These people kneel before the cross and place their guilt, their worries, their pain and their fears before the Savior. Their faces are radiant and they are beautiful—they are marked with the sign of the cross—the empty cross. They bless the room that they are in and heal hearts.

"Lord, Jesus, teach me to share Your joy freely. Amen."

WOMEN IN BLACK?

I was comfortably seated in an airplane waiting for takeoff. Over the speaker system the pilot added a personal note to his general welcome. "I spent six years in the Air Force and twenty-four years flying with Delta. I want to assure you that my crew and I will do all in our power to make your flight comfortable and safe."

Six months earlier, I had been working for the Air Force hotel in Germany so his reference to his service got my attention. I realized he wasn't talking from his cockpit but right at the front of the coach section. In addition to offering us reassurance, his words worked in another way, forming a beautiful frame around my weeklong trip to California to be with my mom, still vibrant and beautiful. We drove 1,260 miles roundtrip from Escondido to Santa Rosa to attend the memorial service of my mother's sister who had died of cancer after a short illness. During those many miles, we had a lot of time to talk, something we hadn't been able to do for years, which made hours seem to speed by. I didn't even feel tired after the ten-hour drive—amazing considering my tendency to doze when riding and sometimes while driving a car.

Although the memorial service was solemn, I didn't feel the grief others felt. I remembered Aunt M as a woman who enjoyed bright colors, loved to laugh, and never let any dust gather under her feet. She had traveled the world with her church group up to a year before her death. It wasn't a surprise when at her memorial service a line of women clad in purple marched by. Her friends were not going to be caught wearing black for that occasion! Through tears and laughter they celebrated her life and beauty as we did. I regret admitting that there were times earlier that year that I had hesitated to call her because I was afraid to talk to someone so terminal. She'd answer the phone with a cheery, "Well, hello, Hon, how are ya?" Each time I finished talking to her I had a warm feeling all over. She helped me realize that a lady can live and die with dignity.

In Santa Rosa we were only an hour's drive from Pacific Union College and Elmshaven, so on our way home we detoured over the hills to visit some long lost friends. We didn't check to see if they were home but just kept driving, up one mountain and down the next right into beautiful sunshine. Grape vineyards glistened with droplets of rain, and the expanding blue sky made room in my heart for another memory. After a few twists and turns we were in the driveway of a most impressive older home. It was white, gingerbread-style, with a rich green lawn encircling it. Thankfully, my friend Carol was there, with her husband, Bob, our former pastor in New Jersey. After catching up on the news, Carol led a tour of the house of which they were caretakers.

This was no ordinary two-story house. The famous author and early pioneer of the Adventist Church, Ellen White, had lived there for the last few years of her life. We went to a corner room where Ellen had visions, entertained by angels, and wrote more books than I had ever read.

Carol told us several stories about Ellen while she lived there, but there's one description I just have to share with you. Someone described her as "the little woman in black who spoke so lovingly of Jesus." *Wow, I thought, what a tribute— what a wonderful way to be remembered.*

Later, homeward bound on the airliner watching the Mississippi River twist and turn below me, I relaxed and thought of the women who had touched my heart that week. All could have worn black considering the circumstances. In a way, actually, none of them really did, not even Ellen White—not a morose black, I mean. The Savior had lived in each of their hearts, and I saw them as daughters of God wearing the colors of the rainbow that encircles the throne of heaven.

My prayer as each day unfolds is that I'll grow closer to God, learn to laugh at myself, encourage others to walk with a skip in their step, always to wear the colors of heaven—and, last but not least, speak lovingly of Jesus.

SIPPING FROM GOD'S CUP

"I pray . . . that all of them may be one, Father, just as you are in me and I am in you. May they also be in us so that the world may believe that you have sent me. I have given them the glory that you gave me, that they may be one as we are one."   —*John 17:20–22, NIV*

I smiled to myself while gazing at the photo reminding me of the women's retreat in Mainz that spring. Our little band of laughing women had taken a walk through the city on our way to St. Stephen's Church when we stopped at a large metal statue for a group picture. We'd had such a good time. I longingly wondered when I would be able to join them again.

It had been too long—the 9/11 tragedy, surgery, recuperation, just taking my time and not overdoing it—had kept me away. I wanted to feel better and it seemed taking life at half steps was good medicine. The next day when I was groggily waking up after my midnight shift sleep, I heard the phone ring. Don would have to pick that one up, I mused to myself. I was staying right here in the overstuffed chair, cozy and sleepy. I heard Don's voice, "Oh, she's right here. Would you like to talk to her?"

My old friend Adrienne from Rhein Main Air Base had called to say hello and to invite me to the evening PWOC program. I thought it was a great idea and told Don later, "I think I'll go this time," mustering up a little old-fashioned determination.

But later, as we were returning from another round of Christmas shopping, my good plans started to evaporate. I was tired and still didn't trust myself to drive anywhere after a midnight shift, especially, after my experience a month or so earlier. I was driving home after a midnight shift, fell asleep at the wheel and ran up onto a cement traffic island, all while sound asleep. That was a close call. I went into the house thinking, "I wish I could go with Adrienne, but I don't know where her phone number is." I had decided that I would forget the women's evening Christmas program. "Maybe next time," I said, setting limits for myself again.

Then the phone rang. It was Adrienne and she was inviting me to ride with her. "Good grief, Lord, You are so wonderful!" I really wanted to go but driving was a bit too risky. Now I could go. I gathered up my new purchases and tried them on. I felt a little stronger and the face looking back at me from the mirror was smiling. "I guess I'm ready," I whispered confidently to the mirror.

While walking up the stairwell after reaching Adrienne's home, I realized that since arriving in Germany almost two years ago, I hadn't set foot in any Rhein Main Air Base military residence. The aromas and style of military living revived vivid memories. I felt at home again. We chatted all the way to the meeting. Just talking together was a real treat. Only women understand this!

The evening program at the Wiesbaden Chapel was like water to a parched soul. I imagined myself trudging across the desert, and there, on a shaded oasis, was an abundance of great food and beautiful tea adorning cloth-draped tables. Heavenly aromas filled the room. On our table was a warmly colored manger scene. The pretty dome-shaped symbol of the Baby Jesus with the Madonna and Joseph sat prominently on the table. Other tables had pillar candles, a pile of candy canes, lighted candle trees, festively wrapped presents, bright ornaments, and pearl-decked angels. The participants read Scripture and connected all these things as reminders of God's love and care for us.

We sang Christmas carols standing up. I wanted to sit, but then realized why they always stood. We were praising the King! I could stand for Him! My tea cup and goodies could wait! The room seemed to warm as we sang one Christmas Carol after another.

Finally, we sat down but I didn't need to sit any longer. I had so much to thank Him for. My fatigue had fallen away and I felt as warm as the fresh baked biscuits sitting on my plate. That's what Christian Christmas gatherings are all about—sipping from God's cup!

A GIFT FROM THE HEART

It wasn't Valentine's Day but Christmas time. Don and I were newly married and I wanted to give him something I had bought with my own money. So without much thought I drove off into the sunrise to the blood bank.

After giving a full quart or so of my blood, or so it seemed, I drove over to a store to pick up some goodies. So far I had been able to pull the whole thing off without Don's knowledge. Now, I said to myself, just get home! But just as I was paying for my things at the checkout counter, everything seemed to swirl around me and the room went dark. What seemed like a minute later, I was being coaxed awake and asked where I lived and what my husband's phone number was.

I felt pretty sheepish when I was helped up the steps to our first home just outside of Fort Benning, Georgia. Don was waiting at the front door with a big grin and some advice about eating breakfast and not selling my blood.

That Christmas I presented Don with my first work of art—a red flannel nightshirt, made by yours truly—truly a gift from the heart. Don tried it on and it fit perfectly, though I could tell Don preferred that I stay conscious the next time I went shopping.

I am so thankful that Jesus gave us His blood gift at this time when all hearts turn to love. I'm also thankful for a wonderful husband (since 1970!) and a sweet daughter. Here's His promise: "This is how much God loved the world: He gave his Son, his one and only Son. And this is why: so that no one need be destroyed; by believing in him, anyone can have a whole and lasting life" (John 3:16, The Message).

HAPPY GAS

I was a full grown mother when I came upon the discovery of happy gas at the dentist's office. Usually, I dreaded going to the dentist because I knew I would have to endure another torture treatment of keeping my mouth open (yes!) while the dentist gingerly drilled away. For some reason, my jaw would cramp and then between rolling my eyes and contorting my face I literally begged the dentist in silence to understand that I REALLY needed to take a break. No one in the room ended up happy—until, that is, I discovered that I could end the cycle of pain by breathing in happy gas.

I remember the scene so well. They put a cup-like device over my mouth and asked me to breathe in deeply. In what seemed like a fraction of a second I relaxed and the dentist and his technicians were transformed into misty white shadows speaking in muffled tones that seemed to encourage my funny bone. Before I knew it, the procedure was over and I sat amazed in the waiting room for an obligatory thirty minutes. I had only one more treatment with happy gas because the rest of my dental appointments were back on post where no such luxuries existed. But I did so much better after that. My jaw didn't ache anymore and the time seemed to pass rather quickly. I don't laugh a lot in the dentist chair like I did that great dental day but neither do I dread going anymore.

What do you dread? Is it a trip to the dentist? Moving? Doing taxes? Flying? May I recommend a sort of spiritual aerodynamics that lightens the heart and lifts the spirit. Nehemiah refers to it as the Lord's joy: "The Joy of the LORD is [my] strength [and burden lifter]" (Nehemiah 8:10).

Start training your heart by writing down ten things you are thankful for and then read them aloud and repeat the list throughout the day. Thank God even for the things that burden you now because Jesus can turn any burden inside out and make it a blessing!

TRY TO REMEMBER

*Train up a child in the way he should go: and when he is old, he will not
depart from it.*   —Proverbs 22:6

Whenever the leaves exchange their green coats of summer for the brilliant
hues of autumn and the air grows crisp and cool, my heart races back to my school
days. My family's home on Flower Street in Inglewood, California, was only a
couple of blocks from our church junior academy, which I attended for nine years.

I smile when I recall my daily encounters with the crossing guard. He always
had a warm smile, greeting me by name no matter how busy he was. After that, it
was easy to walk on to my destiny for the day—school.

All our classrooms had two grades together—us and them. My desk was
my oasis, my space, my world. Inside it I kept an array of erasers, rulers, pencils,
sharpeners, notebooks, paper and other seemingly insignificant items.

Each morning after roll call our class would march outside to the flagpole
and repeat the Pledge of Allegiance as Old Glory was hoisted skyward. Then we
would march back into the classroom to tests and quizzes that awaited us. But in
my mind I would linger a while on the steps to breathe in the fresh morning air.
In the distance I could hear the occasional sounds of traffic, but these seemed
distant from my world.

Recess was a high point of any day with games of capture or conquest chal-
lenging us to new heights of physical endurance. My teachers were all good
Christian folk, inspiring us and leading us to Christ. Our fifth-grade teacher,
Marsha Sawzak, opened our eyes to a world of expression. She ignited the spark
that brought words to the tips of our tongues and fingers and opened our hearts
to eternity. We didn't forget.

Times were great back then but to many of us, this was just a staging area for
the glorious future awaiting us like a winning lottery ticket. I dreamed that one
day I would emerge as Grace Kelly's long-lost daughter and would find my prince
on a white horse. Yes, I planned to write books that would change the world.
With those dreams tucked deep in my pocket, each September repeated itself
with a parade of new friends, rooms, programs, teachers and challenges. The old
school, however, stood alone like a rock, a symbol of permanence and security.

I attended most of the class reunions at Lynwood Academy, but when the
fortieth anniversary of our graduation came up, I remained at home in the much-
anticipated future. I made breakfast for my prince and smiled at the mirror that
tells me I am surely God's child, if not Miss Kelly's. I winced a bit, wishing I could
be there to see old familiar faces, but thankful that I was there back then. "Thank
You, Mom and Dad." I tossed the words over my shoulder as if they could sprout
wings and travel the three thousand miles home. On the weekend of the reunion,
I walked an extra mile with my little white dog, Missy. (That's as close as I got to
the white horse.) I held my head high in thankfulness for the gift I received in
Christian education. It is a joy just to remember it.

THE GIFT LIVES ON

It's been years since we flew from Germany to Hawaii by way of Canada and California. When we left Deutschland that wintry day we made our way through many security checkpoints at the airport. We laid open our purses, took off our shoes and made like a cross as they frisked us. Some probably would have felt violated but I was grateful that they were still checking each passenger so carefully. I prayed they wouldn't miss the real villains.

The trip by air to California was uneventful. We sat close together, trying to read away the time. To my surprise, when we stopped in Canada we went through U.S. customs. We had to gather all our suitcases and wait in line to be looked over and asked questions. Then we reloaded our bags on a conveyor belt and I suspiciously looked over the employees who were to keep my bags secure.

By the time we were waiting in line again to take another flight, this time to Hawaii, we had gathered a whole crowd of relatives. We stood in the Los Angeles International Airport lobby just outside of Inglewood, which was such a big part of our childhood. The folks in front of us and behind us were familiar faces, of course, but from our point of view, we really were strangers. We didn't have a lot of memories with the majority of our relatives, and here we were going on a flight to an island paradise in 2001, little more than three months since the infamous day of September 11.

I remember I was firmly seated in the Hawaii-bound airline, looking over my shoulder for Den's gang, Gary's gang, and Mom and Dad. I wondered what happened to our Steph, who had quickly assimilated with her age group. There were so many thoughts rushing through my mind like cars on a freeway.

My first goals however, were to get warm, to lie on the beach and just soak in the sunshine—something that was in short supply in Germany. We got situated in our hotel room, and then ventured onto the balcony which looked out on the army of roofs below. I knew the beach was out there somewhere.

Day one merged into day two, then day three. We walked the streets, bought trinkets, took trips to the military base, ate pineapple, soaked in the sun, and viewed the gigantic crashing surf. We held family gatherings and rubbed shoulders with brothers and sisters-in-law, nieces and nephews, friends and, of course, Mom and Dad.

We crowded into our rented PT Cruiser and toured the island, including a military cemetery high up on the hill. The crowning event of the day was a celebration and rededication of the folks' marriage of sixty-five years! They appeared almost like newlyweds to my tear-stained eyes. I felt like I was guzzling down more than I could swallow but enjoying every gulp of fellowship, memories and the current surroundings. The air was charged with the warmth of paradise.

As I look back on that 2001 Christmas on Hawaii's shores and try to capture what was most memorable, I know that it wasn't any single event—the sun, the aroma of fragrant flowers or the powerful surf. What I gained from this wonderful holiday together was a new appreciation and friendship with my brothers and their families. I have a mental picture of them and feel closer to them than ever before.

What our folks did to make this possible was no small gift. They worked hard to make it enjoyable. We gathered together as family. What I carry in my heart as a sort of medallion of the entire family vacation was the last scene where we were together—taking the shuttle bus from LAX to our hotel. Our time was almost over. Only our family was aboard the bus, and as we traveled along the streets we knew well so long ago in Inglewood, I heard laughter and talking. Family members who usually didn't get to sit together were seated comfortably beside each other. I saw Mom and Dad sitting together as the captain and his mate at the helm of our ship and thanked God for them and their generous Christmas gift.

Notes on . . .

The Faithfulness of God

In Keeping His Promises
In Speaking to Our Hearts
In Renewing Our Strength
To Dwell in the Hearts of Believers

THE MIDNIGHT CUP

Consider it a sheer gift, friends, when tests and challenges come at you from all sides. . . . So don't try to get out of anything prematurely. . . . If you don't know what you're doing, pray to the Father. He loves to help. You'll get his help, and won't be condescended to when you ask for it. Ask boldly, believingly, without a second thought. —James 1:2–6, The Message

I was sleeping soundly that night in Atlanta, Georgia. My husband, Don, was a ministerial intern and I fell asleep quickly. Then, without warning, I found myself wide-awake and strangely refreshed. I sat up and put my feet flat on the floor, curiously scanning the room to understand what had awakened me. It was 2:30 A.M. Suddenly, the phone beside my bed rang and on the line was a woman in distress.

Although I wasn't acquainted with Frances, words of comfort and assurance came easily. I felt that God was talking through me, using me to minister to that dear sister. She was very depressed, possibly even suicidal. I had no experience dealing with this type of situation but I felt no hesitation and continued sharing with her, filling her midnight cup of woe with His words.

As I look back on that late night conversation, I just laugh at the wonder of it all. Right there in my bedroom, I had been a part of a blessed event. The King of the universe reached down and lifted the burdens of one of His daughters through me.

Ordinarily, when someone calls and awakens me in the middle of the night, from the U.S.A., for instance, I have to struggle to say anything coherent or understandable. I can't think; I slur my words. I'm sure many of you have experienced this if you have friends or relatives living somewhere on the other side of the globe who have awakened you out of a deep sleep. But this time, I felt so refreshed and of course, these words weren't mine, but His. They were God's message to Frances to comfort her that dark night.

Perhaps you have wondered how you could ever bring any kind of spiritual help to someone else. I know that feeling. But you can take time with God. Pull up a chair for Him and talk together. Read His letters. Sit still and listen to Him sing to you.

An unknown author said it so perfectly: "Every morning lean thine arms awhile upon the window sill of heaven and gaze upon thy Lord. Then, with the vision in thy heart, turn strong to meet thy day."

Let Jesus fill your cup and He will! Don't fret about whether you will be able to handle an important situation; just take every opportunity to be bathed in the light of heaven and Jesus will speak through you.

LETTER TO SMOKEY

Dear "Smokey,"

Today I want to thank God for you. This is a time of Thanksgiving but what you said in your last letter really hit home with me and made me realize just how blessed we both are.

It is so easy for us lifelong Adventists to feel we've missed something because we haven't experienced miracles like some who have been out in the world and then found Jesus. But, we can. He wants to work through us and He will work through you, Smokey.

The difference is that our whole lives we heard the stories of the Bible and the good news, so how good could it be—for that matter, could it even be news? But it's not about information, it's about Jesus. When I said, "He is beside you right now," and I believe that with all my heart, I based it on the fact that you are feeling empty. I believe that if Jesus were far from you, you would feel no need. You would be satisfied, filled up with the nothings of this world and be like the lobster in the pan of heating water, not suspecting a thing until it was too late. But you feel your need and you feel that because He is there, His Holy Spirit is opening your heart to Him. Let me share something with you.

"I'm absolutely convinced that nothing—nothing living or dead, angelic or demonic, today or tomorrow, high or low, thinkable or unthinkable—absolutely nothing can get between us and God's love because of the way that Jesus our Master has embraced us" (Romans 8:38, 39, The Message).

So what He offers you is hope! Forever hope. But how do you take hold of that hope? You know, I believe that whatever you're facing in your home in the Smokies, you can know a freedom of spirit and soul right where you are.

Would you do something for yourself?

1. Close your eyes and reach out, open your hands.

2. Ask Him to come into your heart. (See, He's been standing there beside you, but now He wants to be a part of you.)

3. Now, close those hands and draw them to yourself (you are holding His Gift).

4. Now repeat after me, "Thank You, Lord, for the gift of Your precious Son, Jesus."

5. Now, with all of your heart, start talking to Him, tell Him you love Him, that you know He died on the cross for you, and that you want to feel the freedom that only Christians feel.

Now your assignment:

Write down what you are thankful for. Start with simple thing like the nose on your face (wow, think about it, without that nose you'd look awfully silly), then mention the air or the sun or the rain; keep going until you have ten things (at least).

Do this every day for a week in a journal, or notebook or something you can keep together.

Write down promises that are special to you—perhaps John 7:37, 38; Romans 8:14, 15; Romans 5:8-10; Acts 1:8; and Philippians 1:6.

Memorize them and let the power of God flow through these words from you Heavenly Father.

Expect a miracle!

Look for Him everywhere you go.

Ask Him to make you a blessing for others.

(Name), I am asking God to bless you with His presence and peace,

Thank Him before you feel it. Then the feeling will come. It will; I know it will.

NO SHORTCUTS

But those who wait for the Lord [who expect, look for, and hope in Him] shall change and renew their strength and power; they shall lift their wings and mount up [close to God] as eagles [mount up to the sun]; they shall run and not be weary, they shall walk and not faint or become tired.
—Isaiah 40:31, AMP

"Ha!" I laughed out loud at my little dog. "So you won't settle for the cheap way out!" Even though I had held the back door open wide, Missy sat glued to the top of the lounge chair. She was holding out for something better—a walk in the neighborhood with me!

A few moments earlier, I had been sitting on the side of my bed putting on my socks and Missy had been jumping up and down with anticipation. She seemed sure that a morning walk was just around the corner.

But as it too often happens, I got sidetracked and in my haste to get several things done at once, I had opened the door to let Missy out while I fixed breakfast.

When Missy would have nothing to do with that, I realized that my little twelve-pound dog was wiser than I was. She preferred to wait and walk with her master than to go out on her own.

Isaiah penned it well: "They that wait upon the Lord shall renew their strength."

"Dear Lord," I earnestly prayed, "help me to remember not to settle for the fast way out but to walk with You each morning. No backdoor shortcuts for me!"

MY FATHER'S WORLD

> *The earth is the LORD's, and the fulness thereof; the world, and they that*
> *dwell therein.* —Psalm 24:1

The other day I was just starting on an afternoon walk with my little dog Missy, thankful I finally could get outside after such a stormy day. I looked up at the sky and caught my breath. Up there were two huge thunderclouds piled up together. One was coal black and the other behind it was snow white.

As I continued down the sidewalk the two clouds blended together with streaks of black and white weaving a new design in the sky. Then behind the twin clouds the sky began glowing with the intensity of a precious jewel. It looked to me like a blue silk pillow cradling a cameo of God's creation. My heart skipped a beat as I realized I was glimpsing a portion of God's majesty, a small reminder of His faithfulness to my family and me.

Whenever we celebrate Father's Day my mind goes back to what I know about my own human father's world. My Dad was born on a California farm in 1918, the second of seven children. The first years of Dad's life he spoke only German with his brothers and sisters as Grandma and Grandpa were children of a tightly woven community of German immigrants from Russia.

As Dad grew up he enjoyed the many adventures of Boy Scouts, attaining their highest honor of Eagle Scout at an early age. About that time, between the two world wars, when Dad was around twelve years of age he began training the neighborhood boys in military maneuvers, thus starting up his own junior army, with a weekly radio broadcast to boot.

As his interest grew in military matters his parents decided to enroll him in an academy in the southern part of the state. There he developed his journalism skills, learned to eat three square military meals, and practiced military parade marches, among other routine academic activities. Then he met a sweet, curly-haired girl named Nancy and his perspective on life changed radically. Before long Mom and Dad got married and four children followed in royal succession.

In later years, while we were still young, Dad would drive us all down to the ocean by Carlsbad to visit his beloved alma mater, the Army Navy Academy. Its Spanish architecture and the smartly dressed cadets passing by made a lasting impression on this little girl. I guess that's where my love for the military was born. I saw honor in those young men.

During summer vacations I worked for Dad full time at his office in the local Chamber of Commerce and was encouraged to develop many skills from the bottom up—janitor to typist to hostess to a mock rival to the executive director.

Dad has always had a couple of mottos for us recruits (also known as his children). He taught us that we should stay as far away from trouble as we could and seek God's will through His Word. During a recent visit with him, Dad shared his secret of making it through troublesome times: "Make it your habit to read the Bible over and over again, Nan," he shared. "It will carry you through and keep you safe."

When Father's Day approaches, I, like you, naturally turn my heart toward my childhood home. I remember all the good times and personal sacrifices of my parents to keep me in Christian schools. I know my dad's world is changing, as it is for all of us. But there is one thing that never changes—God's faithfulness. As a familiar hymn says, "This is my Father's world; O let me ne'er forget . . . of rocks and trees and skies and seas, God is the ruler yet."[15]

THE HUNT

> *They [Greeks] came to Philip . . . with a request. . . . "We would like to see Jesus."*
> —*John 12:21, NIV*

I walked into the airport that day with memories of other travels engulfing me.

I had grown up near the Los Angeles International Airport where our family used to go and stand at the fence beyond the end of the runway to watch those gigantic aerodynamic wonders lift miraculously into the air. We would dream of the day we too would be able to fly to far-away destinations.

On that day, however, it wasn't the planes that filled my thoughts. Instead, I watched the people around me. The ones nearest me on the plane were either quiet and withdrawn or just plain sleepy, so I really didn't have an opportunity to talk with them at all, let alone to talk to them about Jesus.

I was curious where His children were. And I remembered this phrase, *"What you see depends on what you look for,"* so I was on the hunt. I looked for evidence of the presence of Jesus and He opened my eyes to see pieces of His heart in those I would usually ignore. Here are a few of those I studied. They seemed like angels to me, not with lingering halos or drippy white robes. These angels didn't even have wings that I could see. They looked quite ordinary at first.

Before boarding, there was the woman in the waiting area who gave up her privacy by emptying the seat next to her so I could sit down while I waited for my connecting flight. She started talking right away. For a few brief moments she shared about her mother, who had died the week before. I could sense that her heart was full of memories, even though she didn't share them in detail. What she did share was deep down inside—an intangible piece of herself.

Then I inwardly chucked as I watched a little boy carrying a toy helicopter onto the plane. He and his mother ran down the ramp laughing. Later, in the row behind me, I heard him read in the telltale fashion of beginning readers, giving each word equal time and emphasis. I could tell he was proud of himself and I felt him smile, even though I couldn't see his face. It was contagious, you know.

I owe my plane ticket to the lady and her husband in the airport restaurant who asked if they could sit at my table. Her husband questioned her in detail about what she wanted to eat, which caught my attention. After he left to get their food, she asked me about the time change in Arizona, causing me to realize suddenly that my two-hour layover was in reality only an hour and I had very little time left to get to the gate on the other side of the airport. If I had missed the flight, my ticket would have been forfeited. Because I had to hurry I had only a brief time to study the woman's face, but in it I saw a kindness that still lingers in my memory. It was radiant like an angel!

What I learn from my observations is precious to me. It warms my heart, makes me grateful to be alive, and keeps me coming back to the Bible for another look into the faithful heart of God. From the lady who gave me her seat and memories, I learned that Jesus abides in the precious memories of those we love. From the little boy reading a story, I learned that Jesus loves to share our prayers out loud to His Father. And from the lady who shared my table, I learned that beauty radiates from the heart of a Christian, the ultimate in extreme makeovers.

If we look for Him we can see Him. Abide with me, dear Jesus!

Notes on . . .

Answered Prayer

For Healing
For Added Strength
For Wisdom and Discernment
For Help in Difficult Circumstances
For Grace When the Answer Is "No"

MOUNTAIN PRAYER

"For I am the LORD, your God, who takes hold of your right hand and says to you, Do not fear; I will help you." —Isaiah 41:13, NIV

"Here, let me help you, Steve!" I offered as I reached down to grab the hand of my little brother who could barely reach the guide wires on the steep mountain slope. We had been walking all morning, trudging steadily up the back of Yosemite National Park's Half Dome and were almost there. It wasn't often that my brother, seven years my junior, would yield to any assistance, but his enthusiasm to reach the mountain top erased any fear.

A few more steps and we were standing on the crest of this noble granite sentinel. We stood there out of breath, soaking in the sun and the mountain view of the valley and hills beyond. Without a word, I found a secure area to rest in and relaxed on the cool, hard stone, not wanting to leave.

My youthful mind captured that moment and kept it to this day. I'm not so sure I have the same energy to conquer another mountain peak but as the difficulties of life come knocking at my door I realize just how much I need the Savior's hand to keep going. So it is with any who seek to share Jesus Christ. We are eager to meet our own goals but the really hard things reveal the heart: Loving others when they are unlovable; seeking healing beyond our own needs; and pausing long enough to share the sunshine of His unmerited mercy.

Mountains can be unforgiving in the quest to conquer them. They can also be merciful in the shade they share with weary travelers. The hands that reach out to lift another up are truly God's hand of mercy.

A friend once shared this prayer that is fitting for any mountain we face: "Lord Jesus, keep them going!"

SPINNING MIRACLES

If you don't know what you're doing, pray to the Father. He loves to help.

*You'll get his help, and won't be condescended to when you ask for it. Ask
boldly, believingly, without a second thought.* —James 1:5, The Message

I wheeled the grocery cart around the corner just in time to let out a muted
scream. How many more times would well-meaning people keep asking us when
we were going to have children? Don and I had been married for twelve years
and were really quite content.

That evening at bedtime I knelt and prayed a short but earnest prayer:
*Dear Lord, if You want us to have children, make it plain. If You don't, make that
plain too. In Jesus' name, Amen.* Then I went to bed with no idea of the big plans
already unfolding. I had a strong assurance, however, that this was now in God's
hands. What I didn't know was that He had already begun to spin a miracle,
preparing my heart in so many ways: the lady in the supermarket, my bedside
prayer, and even a gift under the Christmas tree. We had been collecting Precious
Memories figurines for several years and that year, one of Don's gifts was a figu-
rine of a boy and girl holding an open book on their laps with the words "Unto
us a child is born" on the visible page.

I began to be aware of strange emotions growing within me. Both Don and I
felt lonely at Christmas that year for the first time. Being just a twosome seemed
to be losing some of its appeal. I didn't dwell on it until we got a telephone call
one morning in January from an old friend and pastor's wife, whom I'll call Greta,
who said she couldn't get us off her mind. Her unwed daughter, she confided, was
pregnant and wanted to offer the baby for adoption to a Christian home.

Greta and I had met a year before at a conference for the military chaplaincy in Oklahoma. As we were saying our goodbyes in the parking lot, she put
her arm around me and whispered excitedly, "When you get to heaven, God is
going to lay a baby in your arms." That was a sweet blessing, I thought, but I was
content with the way things were—just Don and I on the road again.

When Greta called, I knew something miraculous was happening. Along
with the supermarket encounter, my prayer, the Christmas gift, strange new
emotions, now came the offer of a child. To be truthful, I didn't really think I
would make a good mother. I had never liked babysitting and I really enjoyed the
freedom of our twosome.

But I asked a close friend, I'll call her Faye, what she thought. She was a good
mother and I figured she'd know a good mother-to-be when she saw one. She
assured me I was a good candidate, so after much discussion and prayer, Don
and I agreed to adopt the baby when it was born.

The next few months passed silently. Then Greta called again. "You'd better
sit down," she cautioned. Then she said, "You have a beautiful baby girl!" As soon
as we could get ready we sped in our VW van from Oklahoma to Georgia to pick
up our blessed event. That was more than thirty years ago. Stephanie is now a
college graduate, and we wouldn't trade her or parenthood for anything. It hasn't
been a piece of cake. Children can humble us in ways only God understands. But

I know this: God was leading me and preparing me even before I asked Him. He loved Stephanie even before she had fingernails or eyelashes. He knew her and He knew us and I know He has great plans for her.

Although I didn't physically give birth, I can relate in a way to Mary, the mother of Jesus because God touched me too. I asked Him to make my path clear, and He answered. In essence, he said, "If you don't know what you're doing, ask Me. I love to help."

Thank You, Lord Jesus!

A REBUKE FROM THE GRAVE

"What's with the face, Nancy?" I opened my eyes in amazement to be receiving any kind of letter from my former speech teacher, Dr. George. But this kind of letter, delivered forty years after I had last sat in his college class, seemed surreal.

There was a short note attached to his letter from a member of the family. "After Dad died I found this letter addressed to you lying on his dresser. I thought you would like to have it."

I read on with a funny feeling in my throat: "I know you can do more than that, Nancy! . . . Those songs are about the joy in Jesus. SHOW HIS JOY!"

At first I was a little offended by my professor's criticism of my conduct in a crusade video and I just let his words simmer in the back of my mind. Then, I began thinking of how often every day I get excited and naturally that excitement shows on my face. Why did I think singing about Jesus was so solemn?

"Help me, Lord!" I pleaded, still not realizing how much this rebuke would change me. I laugh now as I realize that God was just waiting for me to ask Him. Thankfully, God answered that prayer and sent His Holy Spirit to give me a new attitude—a spirit of joy!

What I've noticed since that day has been amazing. The people I sing to are so much more responsive. Some have tears welling up in their eyes, and others smile back as they think of Jesus. What's more, I often feel the joy bubble up inside me as it did the weekend I played the part of one of the heavenly host heralding the resurrection of our Savior. I realize now how powerful a smile is when we sing, for we are a reflection of Jesus—we are His voice!

If you and I sing like the Father is described singing in Zephaniah 3:17, a lot of people will be blessed! "The LORD your God is with you, he is mighty to save. He will take great delight in you, he will quiet you with his love, he will rejoice over you with singing" (NIV).

EXPECT SURPRISES

And we are confident that he hears us whenever we ask for anything that pleases him. And since we know he hears us when we make our requests, we can be sure that he will give us what we ask for. —1 John 5:14, 15, NLT

I sat on the edge of my seat up front as part of a panel at the village church at Andrews University searching my memory for one good answer to prayer. My mind was blank as I tried to ease the pain in my back and neck. "Self," I said silently, "I am batting zero here!"

Then I remembered what I had heard a few years before from Glenn Coon of the ABC Prayer Crusade: "Ask God (Matthew 7:7), Believe He will do it (Mark 11:24), Claim or take hold of His promise (Matthew 21:22)." I turned the pages of my Bible for the appropriate verse. There it was: "Behold, I will bring it health and cure, and I will cure them, and will reveal unto them the abundance of peace and truth" (Jeremiah 33:6).

As other panel participants shared their stories of answered prayer, I put my hand on the Bible promise and silently repeated the verse to myself. Then I breathed a thank you to God, still feeling the neck pain as the congregation turned their eyes toward me. It was my turn to share something.

I told the folks that I had claimed the promise, putting my hand on the words of God and that without feeling any pain leave, I thanked God for answering my prayer. Then I told them what was happening to me at that moment. I was surprised at my words as I was sharing an emerging miracle.

"Friends," I began, "I asked God to remove the pain that I have today, but He said, 'No.' I still hurt but He has given me something I never anticipated; I have a peace that covers the pain."

The afternoon church program ended shortly after that. I went home alone remarkably calm. I had His peace and the pain took a back seat. God had answered my prayer in a way I never dreamed. Once in a while these days, my neck muscles act up after lifting something heavy, but when they do, I sit down and relax in His love and cherish His peace that passes all understanding.

You may have something to ask God about. Open your Bible to one of His promises (2 Peter 1:4; Isaiah 42:16; 1 John 5:16; Isaiah 44:3; Matthew 6:14; Philippians 4:13; Psalm 34:4; Psalm 37:4); put your hand on the words from the Lord and buckle your seatbelt; and thank Him for what He is doing. He loves to answer prayers, so expect surprises! He's faithful; He is your Friend forever.

"If radio's slim fingers can pluck a melody from the night and toss it
   over a continent or sea;
If the lilting notes of a violin are blown across a mountain or city's din,
If songs like crimson notes are culled from the thin blue air,
Why should mortals wonder that God hears and answers prayer?"
—Unknown

GOD GIVES US A SONG

"The LORD your God is with you, he is mighty to save. He will take great delight in you, he will quiet you with his love, he will rejoice over you with singing." —*Zephaniah 3:17, NIV*

It was the darkest of all nights, framed only by the massive buildings on either side as we drove through a military base on the outskirts of Oakland, California. After our goodbyes, I remember watching Don make his way into one of the nameless buildings that just seemed to swallow him up.

We had been married just a little over a year and I clung to the thought that time would pass quickly and we would soon be together again. Don had been drafted in 1969, just months after he had graduated from Andrews University. Uncle Sam's birthday card invited him to take a physical. Don went willingly like his father before him, figuring that since he had a business degree the Army would have the good sense to assign him to an important position somewhere. But he soon found that Uncle had pegged him and a score of other college graduates for the infantry instead.

Many tears and prayers later—actually two years to the day—Don headed overseas with a new job classification. He would be assisting chaplains. His destination was Thailand, not Vietnam, I had thought. Years later, I learned that after leaving me Don flew to the Philippines and on to Saigon, Vietnam, where he worked alongside chaplains in the war zone. He didn't write about where he was however, even though I received a trunk full of blue-lined letters just for me.

Over the next twenty-five years, I grew accustomed to saying goodbye to Don at airports around the world. Of course, there would always be a tinge of sadness but I grew creative in my view on my bachelor status. After all, I now had limitless times at shopping malls and full access to the TV remote and later on, plenty of adventures with our Stephi. The hardest part of being left behind was the nights—those times when I would turn off the lights, pull up the covers, and in the deathly still I prayed, both audibly and silently, for more time with my husband. And praise God, He answered.

I know that there is also an army of other spouses who have gone through the same dark experience—some through the floods of depression, the fire of divorce, and the waters of death. But from the least to the greatest of sorrows, God gives us all a song!

"In shady, green pastures, so rich and so sweet, God leads His dear children along;
> Where the water's cool flow bathes the weary one's feet, God leads His
> dear children along.
Some through the waters, some through the flood, some through the
> fire, but all through the Blood;
Some through great sorrow, but God gives a song, in the night season
> and all the day long."[16]

Whatever your life situation, may God give you a song in the night season and all the day long.

SOLID WATER

Fear not: for I have redeemed thee, I have called thee by thy name; thou

art mine. When thou passest through the waters, I will be with thee:
and through the rivers, they shall not overflow thee: when thou walkest
through the fire, thou shalt not be burned; neither shall the flame kindle
upon thee. For I am the LORD *thy God, the Holy One of Israel, thy*
Saviour. —*Isaiah 43:1–3*

I sat outside on the back swing on a cool autumn day in Tennessee. Colorful leaves lay at my feet like bouquets from God. After several years of dreaming, we were finally entering the military as a chaplain family.

It was a dream come true, a prayer answered, and a book yet unopened. There I sat serenading the chipmunks with a guitar in hand. *The Desire of Ages,* a devotional book about the life of Jesus, lay open to the story about Peter walking on the water. I needed that kind of assurance, I thought to myself. I needed to walk on water!

Why not! It would be five years before I would actually set sail on the Sea of Galilee, but right then, with the birds singing protests, I could see it ALL in my mind's eye: a fierce storm, water pelting my face, calling to Jesus who was literally walking on the waves. I took my first step outside the boat (prophetic, you might say) and then found my feet on solid water.

Continuing to visualize, unbelievably I stepped again, and started to laugh in surprise and wonder. I looked away at my friends in the boat. Boy, would they be talking about this one for a long time!

Oops! I was slipping, sliding, SINKING! "No! No! Save me, Jesus!" I said, and as I looked back at Him He held out His hand and gathered me up in His arms. "I love you, Nancy," He said, hugging me tightly. I looked into His eyes. He was shedding a tear as I hid my face in His dry robes.

"Thank You, Jesus," I prayed, back on the bench in Tennessee. "It's my prayer that I never take my eyes off You again! You certainly haven't taken Yours off me!"

JUST THIS ONCE

Two are better than one, because they have a good return for their work: If
one falls down, his friend can help him up. But pity the man who falls and
has no one to help him up! —*Ecclesiastes 4:9, 10, NIV*

As I look back on it now, it was such a sacred moment. Every Sabbath at church, I would answer the call to come to the altar to pray with other brothers and sisters in Christ, big and small. We would kneel down together on the carpeted steps, sometimes putting our hands or arms around each other and facing Him, no one else. Then there would be a moment of silent prayer and the elder of the day would pray. What beautiful prayers! Music seemed to fill my heart and I went away refreshed!

However, it was those silent prayer times, such as the times when in faith

I presented to God the matter of a house for sale of a friend of mine, that I felt closest to Him. It was as if we were in a conversation, and every week we would pick up the conversation right where we left off.

For weeks and months at that Sabbath altar, I brought this prayer request before God on behalf of my friend, but no one came to buy the house. A year passed and still my friend was stuck with the house, even though her husband was already stationed somewhere else far away. Then my friend and her husband gave up a dream and answered a new call to the ministry. It was then that it happened—the house was sold. There was no more waiting.

The next time I walked up front and knelt below that altar, I stared at my empty hands and said, "Lord, thank You for answering my prayer. I have nothing in my hands this time; please fill them with Your grace, Your strength, Your plans." I smiled inside thinking of how He had answered that prayer all along, but in His time.

Right now, I hold out my hands again. I have someone special to put in there, high and lifted up. You do, too, I'm sure. Everyone has someone who would fit perfectly in the Almighty's hands. We can lift up our loved ones before the Lord and place them in His hands, for He is God and He is good.

Just this once, however, in my silly soul, I would like Him to tear down the curtain of time between His house and mine and give me a little peek into the future. I'd ask Him to give me His blessed assurance that my loved one is nestled tightly in His hands. Sometimes we get so tired and discouraged that we forget who He is and how much He loves to save His children. Our human nature clock ticks loudly in our ears. In faith, knowing Him, we can have that bold assurance that, in His time, He will make everything beautiful. Blessed be the name of the Lord!

Epilogue

In one of the episodes of the long-running television series *M*A*S*H,* Colonel Sherman Potter, a medical doctor who commands the 4077th Mobile Army Surgical Hospital in Korea, is sharing with a colleague his dream of retirement.

"I'm going to have me a small medical office in Hannibal, Missouri, with a sign out front that says 'Old Doc Potter' on one side and 'Gone Fishing' on the other."

That scenario is something of a parallel to what has taken place in the lives of Don and Nancy Troyer since Don's retirement after thirty years in the army, most of them as a member of the Chaplain Corps.

Living in the fifty-five-plus retirement community of Sun Lakes in Banning, California, since full retirement occurred in 2005, their home is surrounded by a golf course and other country club amenities, affording ample opportunities for a variety of social and recreational activities. And these they enjoy on a regular basis.

In February 2010, when they celebrated their fortieth wedding anniversary, Nancy noted that the five-plus years they had been at Sun Lakes is the longest time they had lived in one place in all their lives together.

But being retired from active military duty doesn't mean Don and Nancy have retired from life. Nothing could be further from the truth. Both are avid and talented singers and have been members of the 130-voice Sun Lakes Chorale since shortly after moving there. This group, led by Bob Jensen, presents two weekend concerts a year, one in the spring and the other during the Christmas season.

"We practice every Monday morning for three hours for three months before each concert. In addition, there are one- to two-hour section practices weekly," says Nan, adding, "Up until now I had never sung in a choir. I didn't like the strain it put on my voice, even though I love to sing. I always sang solos, or duets with Don, but this was different. We could sing together, even though we aren't in the same section. Don sings baritone, and I have joined the tenor section, a large group of older women whose voices had fallen—along with other things."

Don also sings baritone in a Christian men's chorus called "His Voice," directed by Michael Naluai. They practice weekly and share Jesus in monthly concerts at various churches, senior centers, and prisons in Southern California.

"I am the editor of *His Voice News,* both for their picture journal online at www.hisvoicenews.blogspot.com and their monthly newsletter, shown at www.hisvoice.us. I enjoy being an amateur photo journalist and getting to share in their joy on concert days," says Nancy, who points out that while Don was in seminary they were invited to join one of the touring groups of the Heritage Singers.

"But we decided to continue on the path to the military chaplaincy, so we had to turn down the invitation. But now we can do some of that. I still wish I could sing in a Christian group with Don, but I have been content with singing through the words I write describing God's footsteps through the lives of these fine Christian men in His Voice."

Nancy's musical talent is not confined to singing. She plays the guitar and is the composer of numerous gospel songs, some of which are included on a CD titled *Joyful Songs*. The CD was produced by the Video Evangelism wing of the late revivalist Glenn Coon's ABC Prayer Crusade Ministry

Nancy's artistry in photography is not limited to her journalistic work for His Voice. She loves to take pictures of flowers, of which she and Don have an abundance in their yard. She has an album of her best works, some of which are posted on her Facebook site along with twenty other albums of photos on various subjects. The flowers album includes photographs from her own garden as well as from other locations, including the famed Butchart Gardens on Vancouver Island off the Canadian west coast. Many of the pictures are of salon quality, worthy of publication and gallery display.

Another of her nonadvertised talents is described in the caption of one of her twenty-one Facebook albums, which says, "Nancy took up calligraphy in the early 1980s at Fort Sill, Oklahoma, and with the encouragement of her teacher, she branched out into a different style of calligraphy that she dubbed 'Scribe Art.' She made butterfly cards and sold them at Callaway Garden's Butterfly Museum and military chapels with words outlining the structures. In the 1990s, she added to her Scribe Art collection with "Cool Cowgirl Cards" with Cactus Girl line drawings. This part of her creative nature is in hiatus for now. She may some day revive some part of this art but for now, she'll just post the oldies on Facebook."

While Nancy and Don are extremely busy with their musical activities, they don't neglect opportunities for travel and other recreation. They have taken several cruises and tours and, as she points out in the article "Snow Moon" in the Notes section of this book, ever since their "first honeymoon" on their first anniversary in 1971, they make it a point to celebrate their lasting love with a new "honeymoon" every February 14.

Nancy's busy schedule has not ruled out regular weekly visits with her parents who live approximately seventy miles south of Banning in Escondido. The Neuharths, both in their nineties, celebrated their seventieth wedding anniversary in December 2006. Shortly before that, her mother suffered a fractured hip and other injuries that confined her to a wheelchair.

Midyear in 2010, her mother, whose first name also is Nancy, went to live in her daughter's home as the preferred alternative to entering into assisted living arrangements.

Still later in the year 2010, Nancy's mother suffered a debilitating stroke, making it necessary to move her to a small group care home in Escondido because her medical needs became greater than the family care-giving team was equipped to provide. She went to her rest on December 4, 2010.

"I miss Mom's smile," Nancy says. " Even when she was in a sleep state the last few weeks of her life, she brought peace to the room that covered my heart. When I was gathering her photos for her memorial video presentation, I found so many pictures filled with laughter and smiles. It is calming to know we will see her again and I have a feeling Jesus will be hanging out with Mom. Just a guess, because she had His smile.

"Thinking of Mom and how God worked through her comes clearer each day. I think we all took her for granted because she was such a rock, even in the last months of her life. Now that she is tucked in Jesus' heart, I have time to savor the moments we had together."

Coupled with the responsibility added by her mother's illness, Don's health care also became an issue when it was necessary for him to have two thyroid surgical procedures. He continued to sing with His Voice and the Sun Lakes Barbershop Choir, but felt his voice had not regained its full strength.

To make this update of the Troyers' post-retirement era complete, two other members of the family must be mentioned.

Daughter Stephanie, "Steph," enrolled at La Sierra University in Riverside, California, after coming here from Georgia in 2005, having spent the previous year in college studies in Germany as an exchange student of Southern Adventist University. She graduated from H. H. Arnold High School in Wiesbaden, Germany, before they returned to the United States in 2002.

She received her Bachelor of Arts Degree with a major in English Literature and a minor in German from La Sierra in 2009. After graduation, Steph and Kate Wagner moved to Kentucky where Kate is a doctoral student and Steph retrained and earned national certification as an Emergency Medical Technician and is now working in that field.

Missy #2, the Troyers' Bichon Bolo (for Bolognese) dog, mentioned in the prologue, has made the transition from Germany to California in fine fashion.

"She never tries to run away," Nancy says. "Once since we moved to Sun Lakes we left the garage door open just a crack to allow a nice breeze to circulate through the house and took a walk without her. She didn't care for that at all. She found her way out the garage door opening but ended up waiting for us at the front door."

Missy, who weighs thirteen pounds, has bonded to Don, says Nancy, "but she is my personal trainer. She gets me out on walks around the neighborhood two times a day, early morning and dusk."

It was Don's idea to do a repeat on the dogs' names (you'll remember from